Nietzsche

Nietzsche

Stefan Zweig

Translated by Will Stone

Published by Hesperus Press Limited
28 Mortimer Street, London W1W 7RD
www.hesperuspress.com

First published in German, 1925
This translation first published by Hesperus Press Limited, 2013
Translation and introduction © Will Stone, 2013
Photographs © Will Stone, 2013

The right of Will Stone to be identified as the Author of the Work has been
asserted by him in accordance with the Copyright, Designs and Patents Act
1988.

Designed and typeset by Fraser Muggeridge studio
Printed and bound in Italy by 🦁 Grafica Veneta

ISBN: 978-1-84391-383-2

Contents

Nietzsche during his professorship in Basel

Introduction

My relationship with the present age is from now on
to be war of knives.

– Friedrich Nietzsche

Stefan Zweig's essay on Nietzsche constitutes the third part
of a trilogy within a trilogy, a vivid and impassioned psycho-
biographical exploration of one major figure within a group
of globally renowned artists who had decisively influenced
Zweig's own spiritual trajectory, or with whom he had travelled across his maturing literary life in a protracted fraternal
kinship. As in his other profiles of more modest length, dedicated to numerous artists, writers and musicians, many of
which have never been translated into English, Zweig employs
the same deft psychical probing and an almost febrile passion
for unearthing his subject's inward anxieties and necessarily
thwarted ambitions, the very skills that entranced so many
readers of his fiction both in his lifetime and to the present
day. Through the 1920s, at regular intervals, Zweig published
successive installments of these trilogies to be known as *Die
Baumeister der Welt,* which in English became known as the
Master Builders series. Each triumvirate was selected due to an
espoused spiritual or visionary commonality, a correspondence
of temperament or psychology. The first of these, *Drei Meister*
(Three Masters) (1920), comprised Balzac, Dickens and Dostoyevsky, then came *Der Kampf mit dem Dämon* (The Struggle
with the Demon) (1925), focusing on Hölderlin, Kleist and
Nietzsche, and finally *Drei Dichter ihres Lebens* or (Adepts in
Self-Portraiture) (1928), which turned to Casanova, Stendhal
and Tolstoy. The whole series was then assembled and published as one in 1935. *The Struggle with the Demon* appeared

in English for the first time in 1939, at a moment of great upheaval and uncertainty for its author as Europe prepared to face Hitler's threat. One name notably absent from this list of literary grandees is that of Montaigne, whom Zweig only properly absorbed in exile in Brazil at the end of his life, when, in a desperate search for mental sustenance, he stumbled on a copy of the essays. Had he come to Montaigne earlier it would seem inconceivable, given his eleventh hour reverence for the great essayist, that he would not have been included. Zweig's last literary 'portrait' essay was in fact dedicated to Montaigne, whose eloquent thoughts on suicide and nobleness, notably in the essay 'A Custom of the Isle of Cea', crucially influenced Zweig's decision to take his own life.

Of the three trilogies, it is arguably those peculiarly extreme demands foisted on the tortured spirits depicted in *The Struggle with the Demon* that make it appear the most compelling and relevant to a contemporary audience, perhaps too because the three spirits selected represent an artistic and intellectual phenomenon at odds with the seemingly restrained and financially secure existence of Zweig himself and what appears to be the incremental literary advancement of a prolific 'man of letters'. Having said this, inwardly Zweig himself was no stranger to his own demon, that of angst, periodic bouts of withering depression and a latent suicidal impulse, a preoccupation that perennially leaked into the trajectories of his fictional characters and eventually crystallized in his own demise. Though it should be remembered that Zweig in contrast to outward appearances, never considered himself a calmly advancing, measured person, but quite the opposite, a man afflicted by delirious passions and anxieties which he could barely restrain. This dichotomy between Zweig's inner propensity to morbid despair and his outward appearance of composure, personal warmth and his qualities as a literary statesman and spokesman only heightened the shock, outrage and disbelief at his suicide in Petropolis in February 1942.

Zweig has, not unsurprisingly, been criticised for elements of hagiography in some of his biographies and a glance at portions of rhetorically exultant prose makes such a criticism inevitable. It is true that, especially in his early biographies of those he revered, such as the Belgian poet Emile Verhaeren, or the French writer Romain Rolland, these works might appear today as mere indulgent opportunities to lavish praise on these chosen overseers of Zweig's own spiritual odyssey for their perceived literary 'purity'. But if one looks closer at such 'biographies', which are in fact nothing of the kind, but more ardently persuasive romantic hymns to their subject, there are secreted between the hot-blooded lines numerous subtle insights and valuable discernments which have only managed to germinate and peep through the undergrowth of emotion by drawing an unlikely nutrition from the relentlessly pounding ram of exultation. This juxtaposition of ecstasy and insight forms a key element in the composition of Zweig's typical essay style and is clearly evident in his work on Nietzsche. With Zweig at the controls, the reader must simply strap themselves in and enjoy the ride, taking in the opulent landscapes that appear on either side, the pictorial replenishments offered by Zweig's urgent conviction and obedient imagination. Yes there is repetition; Zweig has a tendency to over-egg the point by reiterating it, but these waves which parade their dauntless energy through the text are all closing in on the one shoreline, in this case to delineate the reality of the fall of Nietzsche in the most plausible terms, and in the most humane manner. Zweig was above all else a humanitarian, who saw culture not as one of numerous tributaries converging on a life richly experienced, but as its main artery, and in Nietzsche he sees not only a complex historical situation involving one great individual of the spirit, but the less resounding tragedy of a solitary misunderstood man hampered by ailments and despair, desperately working for the self realization of a humanity which will always remain blind and fatally harnessed to 'foreground conclusions'.

Does this not then in some sense correspond with Zweig's own personal mission? The noble folly of his ingenuous ideal of European intellectual union and cultural profligacy, in some sense traces the ecstatic crescendo of the great philosopher and the unbearable uninhabited ice floe of its diminuendo. Of course, Nietzsche's ambitions are far more complex, but there is enough symbolic kinship here for Zweig to place Nietzsche as the obvious presiding father of the serviceable current stock of 'good Europeans'. For it was these single-minded, pure intentioned leaders, these noble men of sacrifice, these men of 'example', of whom Nietzsche was but one, which Zweig revered. But Zweig not only supported these dead 'masters' by applauding their exploits and delineating their natures in books; he physically supported one still living by actively promoting his work in Germany on a grand scale. This was the case with the Belgian poet Emile Verhaeren, who was barely known in Germany before Zweig, with customary zeal, determined to address the issue. Still then in his mid twenties, Zweig translated Verhaeren's poetry and pushed his works and personality vigorously into the domain of German letters, organizing lecture tours, readings, and commanding successive editions of the older poet's works. Verhaeren's fame in Germany and his consequent influence on German expressionist poets such as Georg Heym and Jakob van Hoddis, then his export to Russia and hence to the attention of Blok and Mayakovsky, was largely down to Zweig's almost fanatical appreciation of his work, that sense of 'truth' and 'honesty', which the raw, fiery, earth bound voice of Verhaeren symbolized for a young writer keen to leave behind the self-regarding literary cliques and contrivances of the Viennese society into which he had been born.

Zweig is today often acclaimed for his uncanny powers of psychological percipience, especially concerning women, a gift admired by Freud (at whose funeral, in London in 1939, Zweig delivered the oration). Freud recognised the way the threads of Zweig's poised, elegant, yet feverishly backlit prose gradually enmesh and entrance the reader. His strange mixture of patience and raw urgency, of simplicity but erudition, are further contrasting elements which underline the style of his prose, yet this tendency to effuse and rack up superlatives can all too easily appear gauche and over-earnest, leaving a hint of overkill about the text. Is this sense of leaving the ring on too long what made Joseph Roth himself so overheated? Thomas Mann famously grumbled at Zweig's suicide and once testily noted in his diary, 'A deferential letter from Stefan Zweig...' What Mann probably realized but could not bring himself to accept was that Zweig was actually genuine in his deference, and could not help himself, for he actually did believe himself to be a lesser writer than many of his contemporaries. In some sense his 'popular' fame was a thorn to him for he felt that he could never measure up to those 'masters' he was serially infected by. Like many prodigious writers before and since, he suffered anxiety over the value of his own work and its historic permanence. He did not altogether trust the whooping of the literary crowd. Although on the surface he enjoyed success and his popularity was confirmed when, at the height of his fame in around 1935, he was to outsell even a writer like Mann, this left him distinctly uneasy. Apparently controlled and secure, the natural master of pan-European literary ceremonies was also inwardly a hive of discontentment, restlessness, insecurity and sometimes-hazardous indecisiveness. Relentless travel and his repeated expeditions into the heartland of other writers offered some comfort and a renewed sense of commitment.

Zweig's disciple-like passion and single-minded effort to further his ideals was entirely genuine, for it provided a life which lacked any concrete belief system, at least in terms of a religious bulwark, with the authenticity he craved. His relatively privileged position enabled him to take a presiding, constructive role in a European network of like-minded writers and his Salzburg residence through the twenties, when the *Master Builder* studies were written, was awash with international literary guests, the leading artistic lights of the era. Zweig's fundamental concern was to keep track of and personally enthuse a universal brotherhood of those writers and thinkers, both living and dead, he deemed necessary to the continued health of humanity. For example, it is little known that in the summer of 1914, as conflict loomed, Zweig met trusted members of this fraternity to discuss a sumptuous edition of Verhaeren's *Collected Poems* in German. Even Rilke, another Verhaeren acolyte was present. Each was entrusted with a section of the work and was responsible either for performing the translation (as in Zweig's case) or finding a suitable translator. This worthy and ambitious communal project conceived on the eve of the then most destructive war in history symbolises the effort of its leader, Zweig, to advance the cause. But like the premise, the plan was doomed. The edition was never realised, within weeks national borders ossified and Zweig only just made it back to Vienna on the last from Belgium before they were sealed for good.

Zweig's famous autograph and manuscript collection was in some sense a shadowing of his real purpose, which was to imprint the spiritual autographs of the greatest writers on his readership, by unveiling their as yet unexposed fraternal relationships, the threads which bound them together, the movements of the tides within their writings which governed the works reception and appreciation. This profound sense of relating to his subject peaked with the biography of Erasmus of Rotterdam, published in 1935, in whom Zweig saw both spiritual ally and pacifist counterpart, a lone guardian of humanity trapped in his own dark age, facing the cruelty, intolerance, nihilism and lunacy of puritanical religion. For Zweig, the mounting totalitarian threat to his own epoch could all too easily be superimposed on the idea of those massing dark forces defied by the lone flame of Erasmus.

Zweig then was an artist addicted to embracing other artists and securing evidence of their genius, to offer them a place in his growing network of manuscripts, autographs, prints and scores. To this end he could be unusually persistent. Rilke, for one, noted Zweig's countless rather strained attempts to secure an unpublished poem for his collection. Zweig was both instinctively preserving greatness in his collection and irresistibly illuminating it in his biographical profiles. Again and again, as he secured a deep kinship with a writer, he was gladly seduced into the role of servant and spokesman of inwardness for the always more eminent nib. Yet this was not an obsequious lackey-like service to greatness, existing only on the surface, for Zweig was extremely dedicated in terms of penetrating deep into his subject's psyche and yet genuinely regarded himself as a learner before the likes of Dostoyevsky, Tolstoy, Stendhal and Balzac. This 'loyalty' is no more evident than in the account of Nietzsche, which seems somehow to crown the preceding essays, where the demon has almost met its human match in the figure of the stubborn philosopher seasoned with so many circumvented suicides, who goes further into thought than any other being before or since, and due to the fortune of a hearty constitution endures long enough to create something of unprecedented value to humanity.

To Zweig, Nietzsche, what he stood for and achieved, has more about him to worship than any conventional religious deity. But the fact that Nietzsche was a man with all the weaknesses, fears and failures inherent to a human being makes him even more worth revering, because only through a colossal power of the will did he force himself beyond the limits generally imposed by reality. Like many writers and thinkers with one foot in the nineteenth century and one in the twentieth, Zweig revered Nietzsche as the prophet who somehow, despite his blatantly clear message scrawled again and again across the materialist, militarized and science-infatuated last decades of the nineteenth century, could not be prised out in time by his legion future rescuers (such as Zweig) from the colossal 'no reply' and ensuing darkness of his own epoch, the haunted ailing figure who ended his days craven under nursing home blankets staring into the dry well of insanity and death, he who had gambled on a new higher caste of humanity emerging somewhere beyond a rationalist expansionist Germany he could no longer endure. So Nietzsche the prophet was dead, 'hunted down' and killed off by the very people he had sought to guide; Zweig felt a responsibility to serve Nietzsche by truthfully exhibiting him as a tragic figure in the human dimension, as an exceptionally solitary artist with an indomitable will enduring against all the odds, not as the theatrical superhero of modern German mythology, which at the time of writing was the public image to which Nietzsche was increasingly prone. Right from the opening chapter, Zweig attacks the German appropriation of Nietzsche and the ensuing Teutonic embellishments to his figure. It is clear that Zweig is attempting to free Nietzsche from the nationalist creepers that are, with his sister Elisabeth's insidious feeding, ever more powerfully entwining his legacy after the First World War, and to relocate him as the key modern universally relevant 'master builder of the spirit'. Zweig wants the reader to feel what price Nietzsche paid as a man in his time gifted with visionary perception and the strength of will, how, despite possessing the utmost clarity of thought and unclouded integrity, he was ignored and obliged to accept the wooden spoon of only posthumous appreciation. But above all he wishes to show that this was inevitable, given the inability of the German people to be readied for Nietzsche's thought. Beyond this he can say little more. Zweig demonstrates the crime of Nietzsche's neglect by focusing on the failure of a modern industrialized country increasingly harbouring imperialist fantasies, to recognize his warnings, but also the establishment's scholarly establishment is also criticised for its incessant outpourings of volumes, its ever feverish activity, yet its abject failure to notice the one great mind sending up flare after flare in its midst.

Zweig goes on to articulate Nietzsche's coruscating solitude and his infamously nomadic existence, now tinged with a certain melancholy exoticism, the life of a 'fugitive' whose nerves are a delicate barometer registering the surrounding elements and sending the 'outlaw prince' to all corners of the continent in search of the perfect climate in which he might exist more productively. Zweig lists the locations like so many chance oases on the long desert journey of a heavy wool coated vagrant. But it is the high plateau of the Engadine in Switzerland, and the little lakeside village of Sils-Maria, where Nietzsche settled over consecutive summers in the 1880s and wrote certain of his most famous works, that draws Zweig's main attention. Only here could Nietzsche properly breathe, he claimed, due to its 'invigorating and ozone rich air', and he even latterly expressed the wish to build a permanent home on the peninsula. The little nondescript room still preserved today in the Sils house becomes for Zweig the prime martyrdom cell in which the tormented man pursues his path to posthumous greatness. Like many German-language writers and poets drawn since by the shadow of Nietzsche, and of the singular majesty of a landscape that equated with his thought, Zweig had visited the 'Nietzsche house' at Sils-Maria, stayed at the hamlet of Baselgia and made the pilgrimage walk down the Chastè peninsula into the lake at the heart of Silvaplana, taking the same paths Nietzsche would have taken. Yet Zweig, interestingly, suggests a certain malignancy in the casual sightseeing, which the philosopher's name has brought to Sils-Maria. This recalls a preoccupation with the proliferation of tourism on the back of human suffering made explicit in his essay on Ypres (see Stefan Zweig – *Journeys*, Hesperus Press, 2010).

Nietzsche's fixation on climate is bound, Zweig argues, to the mental suffering and intellectual tension experienced during his travels, so that 'Little by little, he distills from his pathological experiences a kind of sanitary cartography for his own personal use.' It is interesting how Zweig marvels at Nietzsche's diverse itineraries and restless criss-crossings of Europe, for of course he too was an insatiable and perennial traveller and was never satisfied in one place for very long. For Zweig, the carriage of a train proved often the least demanding and most creatively fruitful environ in which to locate himself. But as ever the gulf between the relatively secure existence of a writer like Zweig, at least until Hitler came to power, and the precarious voyages to further insight and alienation served by Nietzsche's dauntless thought locomotive, could not be wider. Two of the most influential architects for a European ideal are seen sharing the same tracks and heading for similar Central and Southern European destinations, but in contrasting circumstances and bearing very different loads.

Zweig relishes transmitting not only Nietzsche's mania for climate but also for dietary issues and ailments. He rummages in Nietzsche's travelling trunk for the tragic evidence, which is all too abundant, depicting his creative period as a perennially solitary endurance course, a physical and mental road to perdition amidst the empty bottles of chloral and veronal, where the interchangeable narrow bed in a shabby alpine lodging house is the rack on which he must prostrate himself between bouts of vertiginous writing. Although there is a lush romanticism inherent to Zweig's depictions of Nietzsche, and inevitably the scene becomes the very theatre Zweig seeks to avoid, the portrait is nevertheless vital, suasive and plausibly harrowing in its detail. Zweig focuses heavily on Nietzsche's physical and mental suffering, something which today may be common knowledge and must naturally feature in every biography of him. Yet unlike a dry dispassionate academic biographer, in Zweig's sensitive 'fraternal' hands there is something genuinely moving and innately humane, something almost brilliantly fictional, and yet true when he describes the furtive entrance of the myopic philosopher into a guesthouse as the gong goes for dinner, or his failure to maintain a conventional conversation with a casual acquaintance due to having lost the faculty to do so. It is in the detection and implication of this indifferent reality, these dread struggles, not so much with the demon, but with the real world, the minutiae of everyday life, the life Nietzsche necessarily had to pass through as his vision evolved into literature, that Zweig really excels.

Zweig's take on Nietzsche, or his reason for including him in his demonic triumvirate, is basically that he, like Hölderlin and Kleist before him, was inexorably and helplessly possessed by a 'demon', or was in another sense intoxicated, 'blinded by spirit'. However, he himself makes clear in his introduction that this demon is not the satanic kind, but the fiend dispensing torment to those seeking spiritual anchorage, that seductive yet dangerous elemental yearning to escape from the rational conventional forms of existence and to embrace, as Zweig asserts, 'danger, immoderation, ecstasy, renunciation and even self destruction' in order to reach a higher plane, to exist only in an atmosphere of complete freedom. Zweig views the three chosen artists, who are all German and either fell prey to madness or suicide, as prime examples of this case. Unsurprisingly, he cites Dostoyevsky and Van Gogh as also being in thrall to the demon;

both Dostoyevsky and Van Gogh make their entrance more than once throughout the text, as fraternal shades following Nietzsche on a similar circumnavigation of the abyss. But there is a further artist who is perhaps most crucial to the essay other than Nietzsche himself, another monumental figure Zweig also deeply admired: Goethe, who was diametrically opposed to Nietzsche in virtually every respect. In these two great German heavyweights, Zweig recognised the polarized struggle of every genuine artist, like two giants, their interlocked shadows back lit on a cave wall. He stresses the constant tension between those in the grip of the demon, the force of excess and uncompromising subjectivity that, pied piper-like, leads Nietzsche into his intensely productive yet fatal Dionysian dance, and that of its exact counterpart, carefully tended artistic progress, as represented by Goethe and his 'capitalist' approach, engrossed in the steady accumulation of experience. Laurence Mintz, senior editor of the Transaction Publishing edition of *The Struggle with the Demon* (2011, Translation Eden and Cedar Paul, 1939), sees Hölderlin, Kleist and Nietzsche as those who 'consciously opposed the worldly harmoniousness of Goethe's classicism in favour of a visionary inwardness and dramatization of the subjective psyche'.

This duel between the respective attitudes of Nietzsche and Goethe proves a fascinating sideshow to the essay and provides some extra vertebrae to the backbone proper, the breakthroughs and trials of Nietzsche as he slides ever further down the greasy pole of the half submerged vessel of his life. Clearly Zweig has taken the opportunity to explore this dichotomy between two approaches to art and their resulting gains and losses for the artist concerned. This comparison culminates in the experience of Italy and the south upon the two men, afflicted by the grey lowering skies of the North both literally one presumes and spiritually, and both searching for a new horizon, a way to wrest themselves free of Germany's leaden bonds. But only Nietzsche, in Zweig's view, really achieves a decisive break and the longed-for rebirth. 'Goethe's experience is primarily cerebral and aesthetic whilst that of Nietzsche is vital. Whilst Goethe's first relationship with Italy is of the artistic kind, Nietzsche discovers a new style of life itself. Goethe is simply enriched whilst Nietzsche is re-rooted and renewed.' This 'vitality' represented by the south is for Nietzsche ultimately a further tool to extend his existence to the point of collapse, the famous collapse outside no. 6 via Carlo-Alberto, whose aftermath Zweig dramatises at the close of his portrait in a heady mixture of the genuinely emotional and the precariously theatrical.

The general premise of Zweig's account is how Nietzsche suddenly casts off the old skin of his professorial philologist existence in Basel and embarks for a new life, his real life, or, most importantly for Zweig, the authentic life, and the only one that matters in terms of Nietzsche's relevance as creative artist. It is these fifteen years of suffering and transcendence that Zweig concentrates on, while the Basel period and the final descent into madness in Italy form the outer casing, the necessary germination period and dying back after the productive harvest. Again and again Zweig returns to the 'sterility' of the Basel period, the fossilizing of Nietzsche by academic application and the hoary company of 'experts', then the breaking of the constricting shell, the bursting forth into the sunlit uplands of pure freedom of thought. It is this one tantalizing notion that obsesses Zweig throughout his essay, whatever the inevitable restrictions to his theory reality might plant in his way. Zweig is determined, like a man on a mission himself, to get across this decisive abandonment of security by Nietzsche and his propensity to take an ever more self-destructive tightrope walk, where all safety nets are strictly forbidden. Zweig clearly expounds this Nietzschean stance as heroic whilst 'respectfully' deploring the anti-heroic nature of Goethe, whose life steadily extends 'like the rings of a tree', and who remains to the end in thrall to the establishment.

Zweig celebrates Nietzsche as the supreme 'aeronaut of the spirit', the one who dared, acted and then declared: 'I made the leap!' For Zweig the decision to leap and the actual leaping are what counts, though the landing occurs in downfall, the fact is Nietzsche really did renounce everything for the sake of thought, and did so sensing the cost must be his own life. It is this total rejection of compromise and martyrdom that enthralls Zweig, appealing to that part of him which could never take such decisive action. Nietzsche becomes for Zweig an emotionally inexhaustible fantasy figure, a master of masters who plays out all the most crucial values engendered by the will to their most dizzying extremes. Zweig sees everywhere a potential 'creative configuration' around his subject, for it is the vital progression of Nietzsche's legacy, in spite of his fall, that Zweig, without actually disclosing what that might be, seeks to magnify in his essay. Though today a conceit such as Zweig's 'demon' may sound to us rather quaint and would in the lecture halls of today no doubt be dismissed, the elements of this state as Zweig describes them are clearly recognizable in the artists that he portrays, but are surely most powerfully and supernaturally felt in the figure of Nietzsche, a figure so historically colossal in terms of his thought, but as a single human being so vulnerable and easily crushed by the weight of his epoch. It is not only the passion of Zweig for the titanic nature of his subject, the awe felt before such universally relevant originality of thought, the realization of the devastating effect of such turbulent inner forces on a human being, that is so energetically and imaginatively displayed through these chapters, but the passion for a purity of intention, non artificiality, the fanatical adherence to principle and authenticity, key humanitarian values Zweig always sought in himself and expected to dominate and proliferate, values which were and still are surely decisive as to a generation's worthiness to survive at all.

A Note on the Translation

Although this constitutes the first modern translation of Zweig's essay on Nietzsche, it is not the first, as during Zweig's lifetime Eden and Cedar Paul translated many of Zweig's works, both fiction and non-fiction. Their output was prolific and it was largely through their translations published by the Viking Press that Zweig's name was established in the Anglophone world. Aside from the more obvious biographies of historical figures, the Pauls also concentrated on the *Master Builder* series and it was their version of *The Struggle with the Demon* which was published in 1939 as the second part of the sequence. The Pauls' translations were reissued in the handsome Hallam series of Zweig's works published by Cassell in the 1950s, allowing the next generation access to Zweig's works in English.

The great Zweig drought then existed for decades until the 1990s when Pushkin Press sought to readdress the balance. Pushkin, who have been acknowledged for their central role in the recent Zweig renaissance in the UK, have now released a number of these Eden and Cedar Paul versions in new editions, including *The Struggle with the Demon*. Previously to this development in the summer of 2012, the version was available in a 2011 edition published by Transaction Publishers, edited by Laurence Mintz.

It is my hope that this new translation of the Nietzsche portion of that book may stand alone as a single work, as has been the case in recent years with its appearance as a sole entity in French translation. Although republishing the older English translation was justified, since it was the only existing translation available, the reader will see a notable difference between that text and this one, not only in terms of style, given seven decades have passed, but also content. I have made it my priority to eschew any summarizing technique or dilution of the original text and have retained the content as far as possible line by line, without slavishly reproducing the German structures. Although I have endeavoured to produce, indeed write, a readable and comprehensible 'modern' sounding English and avoided archaisms, I have also tried to stay true to Zweig's distinctive period tone and richly ornamented, highly expressive flourishes. One of the most gratifying aspects of this task was to perform a kind of archaeological restoration on this text and bring up still preserved from the depths what treasures sank with Zweig himself during the war and can now I hope be looked on anew.

– Will Stone

Nietzsche in the Villa Silberblick, Weimar, July 1899

Nietzsche

I think of myself as a philosopher
only in the sense of being able
to set an example

Untimely Meditations

I
Tragedy without a Cast

To profit most from existence, man must live dangerously.

The tragedy of Friedrich Nietzsche is a monodrama: no other figure is present on the brief lived stage of his existence. Across the acts of this tragedy, which crash down and surge on like an avalanche, the isolated combatant stands alone beneath the stormy sky of his own destiny; nobody is alongside him, nobody is opposing him and no woman is there to momentarily relax the overstrung atmosphere with her presence. Every movement issues from him alone and he is its sole witness: the few figures who at the outset linger in his shadow can only accompany his heroic enterprise with gestures of dumb astonishment and alarm and little by little distance themselves from him as if from some danger. Not a single being dare properly enter the inner sanctum of that destiny; always Nietzsche speaks, struggles, suffers for himself alone. He addresses no one and no one responds. Worst of all: no one is even listening.

There are no other people, no fellows, no listeners in this unique tragedy of Friedrich Nietzsche, but neither is there a stage, scenery or costume, for it plays out, so to speak, only in the airless space of the idea. Basel, Naumburg, Nice, Sorrento, Sils-Maria, Genoa, these names were not those of Nietzsche's homes, but merely a series of milestones along a road travelled in a burning flight, the cold colourless wings of the theatre. In truth the scene of this tragedy always remains the same: isolation, solitude, that cruelly wordless responseless solitude that his thought carries within and around itself like an opaque bell-jar, a solitude without flowers or colours, without sounds, animals or people, a solitude deprived even of God, the extinct and stony solitude of some primeval world existing before or beyond time. What makes this desolation so harrowing and ghastly, so truly grotesque, is that this glacier, this desert of solitude occurred at the heart of an Americanized Germany of some seventy million inhabitants, in the rattling and whirring of telegraphs and trains, of cries and tumult, at the centre of a morbidly prurient culture which every year launches forty thousand volumes into the world, that every day searches around a thousand different problems in a hundred universities, that every day stages tragedies in hundreds of theatres, and yet knows nothing, divines nothing and senses nothing of the great drama of the spirit unfolding right in their midst.

For it was precisely at its most sublime moments that the tragedy of Friedrich Nietzsche failed to find spectator, listener, or sole witness in the German world. At the beginning when he is in a position to proclaim from the lofty heights of his professorial lectern and the spotlight of Wagner finds him, his discourse secures a measure of regard. But the deeper he descends inside himself, the more he plunges into the far reaches of time, the less any response is detected. One after another, friends, strangers, stand up shocked, in the course of his heroic monologues, alarmed by the ever more wild transformations, the ever more heated frenzies of horrifying solitude, and abandon him on the stage of his destiny. Little by little the tragic actor becomes agitated at declaiming into a void, so he begins to raise his voice, to shout and gesticulate more wildly to create an echo or at least a contradiction. To harmonise with his words, he invents a surging, intoxicating, Dionysian music – but now no one is listening. He tries a harlequinesque turn, ascribes to a forced gaiety, strident and piercing; he builds into his phrases all manner of twists and turns (mimicking comic improvisations), just to attract through artificial amusements, listeners to his deadly earnest evangel, but no hand is moved to applaud.

Finally he invents a dance, a dance of swords and, butchered, torn, bloodied, he performs his new deadly art to the public, but no one guesses the significance of these shrill jokes, nor the passion wounded to death that exists in this affected light-heartedness. Without listeners or echo, the most extraordinary drama of the spirit ever granted to our troubled century is played out to its bitter end before an empty house. No one turns their glance even cursorily towards him, when the whirligig of his thoughts spinning on a steel point leaps exuberantly for the last time and finally falls, exhausted on the ground – 'Dead by immortality'.

This aloneness with the self, this solitary state of being face to face with the self, is in the deepest sense the exceptional sacred affliction of that tragedy which was Friedrich Nietzsche's existence. Never was such an imposing consummation of the spirit, such an extreme bacchanal of feeling placed before such a colossal void of the world, in the face of such a metallically inviolable silence. Nietzsche never even had the fortune to find worthy adversaries; so the most powerful will of thought, 'closed in on itself and burrowing deep into itself', was obliged to seek out a response and a resistance in his own breast, in his own tragic soul. It wasn't the world, but the bleeding strips of his own skin that this spirit raging with destiny tore away, like Heracles, his Nessus shirt, with that burning desire to be bared before ultimate truth, to confront himself. But what glacial chill accompanies this nakedness, what silence around this cry of the spirit without precedent, what terrible sky crossed by storm clouds and lightning, above this 'God murderer', who now having encountered no adversary turns on his own being, 'Knower of himself, torturer of himself, merciless one'. Hounded by his demon beyond time and the world, beyond even the furthest limits of his being.

Shaken alas! by unknown fevers,
Trembling before airborne icy shafts,
Hunted down by you, oh thought!
Inexpressible! Sinister! Horrifying!

Sometimes he recoils quivering, with a nameless look of terror, when he recognises to what extent his life has rushed beyond all that was living and all that had been. But an impulse so powerful can no longer be restrained: with surging confidence and hugely intoxicated with his own self, he accomplishes the destiny that his beloved Hölderlin had prefigured for him – that of Empedocles.

Heroic landscape devoid of sky, sublime performance without an audience and silence, a silence growing ever more intense around the unbearable cry of this lonely spirit, that is the tragedy of Friedrich Nietzsche. We should abhor them, as the numberless insensate cruelties of nature were it not for the fact that he himself selected and embraced them ecstatically, adoring them for their unique harshness and solely because of that uniqueness. For voluntarily, in all lucidity, renouncing a secure existence, he constructs this 'unconventional life' with the most profound tragic instinct, defying the gods with unrivalled courage, to 'experience himself the highest degree of danger in which a man can live'. 'Χαιρετε δαιυονες! Hail, demons!' It was with this jocular cry of hubris, that once, one evening, in the light hearted manner of students, Nietzsche and his philosopher friends summon up supernatural powers: at the hour when the spirits are abroad, they pour through the open window the red wine from their brimful glasses into the sleepy Basel street as a libation to the unseen, an imaginative jape, but one which harbours a more serious presentiment nonetheless: for the demons hearken to this call and pursue the one who defied them, turning an evening lark into the monumental tragedy of a destiny.

And yet, Nietzsche never shrinks from the colossal demands by which he feels irresistibly seized and drawn: the harder the hammer strikes, the clearer the tone from the bronze anvil of his will. And on this anvil, made red hot from the mighty flame, is forged, ever more powerfully and reinforced with each blow, the watchword which would armour his mind in bronze; 'the greatness of man' *amor fati*: never seeking to change the past, the future, eternity; not to just bear necessity, much less to conceal it, but to love it. This ardent song of love addressed to the spirits, covers like a dithyramb the cry of his own pain: bent to the ground, crushed by the world's silence, eaten up by himself, seared by the bitterness of suffering, never once does he raise his hands to ask of fate to finally forsake him. On the contrary, he demands still greater adversity, deeper solitude, a larger capacity for suffering. Not in defence does he raise his hands, but to launch the glorious prayer of heroes: 'Oh will of my soul, that I call fate, you within me! You above me! Enshrine me and preserve me for a great destiny.'

Whosoever offers up such grandiose prayers must surely be heard.

II
Double Portrait

A theatrical pose does not beget greatness;
whoever strikes an attitude is false. Beware
of all men who appear picturesque!

Theatrical image of the hero. The marmoreal lie set in stone.
The picturesque legend is born, the undaunted heroic head, the
high-vaulted brow riven by dark thoughts, the downward wave
of hair above a proud neck. Beneath bushy eyebrows glitters the
gaze of a falcon; each muscle of this powerful face is tense with
will, health and vigour. The Vercingetorix moustache falls rug-
gedly over a severe mouth and prominent chin, suggesting the
fierce warrior, and involuntarily they couple this powerfully
muscled lion's head to the body of a German Viking advancing
with great strides brandishing the sword of victory, the hunting
horn and lance. That is how, arbitrarily making him into a
German superman, an antique idea of a chained Prometheus,
our sculptors and painters like to present the solitary of the
spirit, to make him more accessible to a humanity with faith
only in schoolbooks and the stage, leaving them only capable
of understanding the nature of the tragedy when it is veiled in
melodrama. However, the true portrait of Nietzsche is much
less picturesque than the busts and paintings made of him might
suggest.

Portrait of the man. The comfortless dining room of a 6 francs
a day pension, a hotel in the Alps or on the coastline of Liguria.
Indifferent guests, most often elderly ladies absorbed in 'small
talk', chitchat. The bell chimes three times to summon the guests
to table. Over the threshold passes a slightly stooped indistinct
figure with sagging shoulders: as if exiting a cave, Nietzsche,

who is 'seven sixths blind', always makes his entrance into a foreign pension with a less than assured step. He is clad in a dark suit, carefully brushed; his face is equally dark, the hair brushed back, brown, wavy. Dark too are the eyes behind the round polished thickness of the invalid's glasses. Gently and timidly he approaches, an imposing soundlessness about his presence. One feels here is a man residing in the shadows, apart from all social conviviality, a man whose neurasthenic anxiety registers the slightest noise: politely, with a refined courtesy, he greets the other guests, who with equal politeness and an amicable indifference, return the German professor their greetings. With the prudence of the short-sighted, he advances towards the table; with the prudence of a man possessing a delicate stomach, he examines every dish: to ensure the tea is not too strong, that the food is not too spiced, for culinary errors will irritate his fragile plumbing and any mistakes made with his food could upset for whole days his quivering nerves. Not a glass of wine, not a glass of beer, no alcohol, no coffee, no cigar, no cigarette to follow the meal; nothing which stimulates, refreshes or relaxes; only a brief and meagre repast, a scattering of urbane conversation, superficial, in a low voice with a chance neighbor (like a man who over the years has lost the habit of social interaction and dreads the prospect of being asked too many questions).

Then he goes back up to his little furnished room, narrow, mean, coldly decorated, the table strewn with countless papers, notes, writings and proofs; but not a flower, not an ornament, barely a book and rarely a letter. Over in the corner stands a large and heavy wooden trunk, his only asset, containing two clean shirts and a fresh suit. Aside from these, only books and manuscripts. On a shelf, innumerable bottles, flasks and tinctures: for headaches, which regularly occupy so many wasted hours, for stomach cramps, spasmodic vomiting, intestinal weakness, and above all, those terrible medicaments to control insomnia – chloral and veronal. A horrifying arsenal of poisons and narcotics – the only help that he can call on in this empty silence of the foreign room, where he finds no other rest but a brief sleep obtained only artificially. Squeezed into his coat, enveloped in a woolen shawl, (for the miserable stove smokes, but gives out no heat), fingers numb, his spectacle lenses hard up against the paper, he forms for hours on end with hurried hand words that the afflicted eyes can barely decipher. For long hours he sits there writing like this, until his eyes burn and shed tears: it is a rare pleasure in his life, when someone pities him and offers to take dictation just for an hour or two. When it is fine, the solitary ventures out, but always alone – always alone with his thoughts: never a greeting en route, never a companion, never an encounter. The bad weather, which he hates, the rain, the snow, that makes his eyes hurt even more, mercilessly keeps him a prisoner in his room: never does he descend to the others, towards humans. In the evening, a few biscuits, a cup of weak tea and then once more that infinite solitude stretching away, alone with his thoughts. For hour after hour, he keeps watch beside the lamp with its unsteady smoky flame, without his feverishly stretched nerves ever gradually releasing into a mild languidness. So his hand clutches at the chloral, any kind of soporific, and then finally, he obtains only brutally a sleep meant for others – for those free of thought, those not hounded by the demon.

Sometimes he spends the whole day confined to bed. Vomiting and cramps until he loses consciousness, searing pain in the temples, sent almost blind. And no one comes to his aid, not even a helping hand, no one to lay a cool compress on his burning brow. No one to read to him, to chat with him, to laugh with him.

And that furnished room is everywhere the same. The towns may change their names, now Sorrento, now Turin, now Venice, now Nice, now Marienbad, but the furnished room always remains the same, always that rented foreign room, with its old, cold, worn out furnishings; with the little writing table and the bed, that rack of pain, and unbroken solitude. Never, during all the long nomadic years, any mirth in a friendly cheerful milieu; never, at night, a warm naked female body beside his own, never a dawn of glory breaking after the thousand dark and silent nights of toil! Oh, how much wider is the solitude of Nietzsche, how infinitely wider than the picturesque high plateau of Sils-Maria, where now the tourist somewhere between lunch and dinner delights in frequenting his domain: his solitude stretches across the entire world and over his own life, from one end to the other.

From time to time, a guest, a stranger, a visitor calls on him. But the crust is now so hard, so unyielding around the yearning, the people-craving kernel: the Solitary breathes again, is relieved, when the stranger leaves him to his solitude. After fifteen years any sense of association is entirely lost. Conversation wearies, exhausts, irritates he who consumes himself, who always hungers for himself. Occasionally, but briefly, a tiny ray of happiness beams. It is 'music' – a performance of Carmen, in a second-rate theatre in Nice, a few arias in a concert, an hour at the piano. But this also brings anguish and 'reduces him to floods of tears'. The privation of joy becomes so deeply entrenched that he can only experience it as something grief-stricken.

For fifteen years this cave life of Nietzsche continues from rented room to rented room, while he remains unknown, with himself alone conscious of his being – this wretched passage in the shadow of great cities, in shabbily furnished rooms, in shelters for the destitute, in grubby train carriages and countless sickrooms, whilst outside, at the surface of time the gaudy circus of the arts and sciences sings itself hoarse: only the flight of Dostoyevsky, almost at the same moment in time, with equitable poverty and neglect, is illuminated by this same cold grey spectral light. Here, as there, the work of a titan conceals the gaunt figure of the poor Lazarus who daily expires from his despair and infirmity in solitude, as day by day, the miracle savior of creative will awakens him from the depths. For fifteen years, Nietzsche emerges thus from the coffin of his room, moving upwards and downwards, with suffering upon suffering, death upon death, resurrection upon resurrection, until, overheated by such a flood of energy, his brain breaks apart. Collapsed on the street strangers discover him, he who was such a stranger to his time. Strangers carry him to the strange room on the Via Carlo-Alberto in Turin. No one bears witness to the death of his mind, as so few were to witness the life of his mind. Around his downfall are darkness and a divine solitude. Unaccompanied and unknown, the most lucid genius of the spirit rushes headlong into his own night.

III
Apologia for Illness

What does not kill me makes me stronger.

Countless are the cries of suffering issuing from the martyred body. It is an index with a hundred entries for every conceivable physical crisis, proceeding to this horrifying final statement. 'At all stages of life, the surplus of pain has in my case been immense.' Indeed no diabolic martyrdom is absent from this nightmarish pandemonium of malady: headaches, pounding and dizzying headaches, which for days leave him prostrate on a couch or a bed in a state of fruitless delirium; stomach cramps, along with vomiting of blood, migraines, fevers, loss of appetite, dejected mood, haemorrhoids, intestinal stagnation, fever shakes, night sweats – a gruesome vicious circle. Add to that 'eyes three quarters lost to darkness' which swell at the least effort or begin to weep and which allow him to enjoy the light for no more than 'an hour and a half a day'. But Nietzsche scorns a healthy body and remains at his writing table for ten hours at a stretch. The overheated brain takes revenge with raging headaches, nervous tension, for in the evening, when the body is exhausted the brain cannot switch off, but continues to pour forth visions and thoughts, until a narcotic must be sought in order to sleep. But he requires ever-greater quantities (in two months, Nietzsche absorbs fifty ounces of Chloral Hydrate, just to snatch a little sleep). Then it's the stomach's turn to refuse to pay such a high price and it revolts. It's a real *circulus vitiosus* – vomiting spasms, fresh headaches, new remedies demanded, the relentless voracious, fervid opposition of overtaxed organs in a mutual exchange with the spiky ball of sufferings. And no respite from this play back and forth! Not the lowest margin of contentment, not the briefest month of pleasure and forgetting of the self; in twenty years, one can count only a dozen letters where a groan does not rise from one line or another. And always more furious, always more violent, becoming the wailings of one who is needled by over-sensitive nerves, too delicate and already over-inflamed. 'So make your lot more easeful; Die!' he cries to himself; or 'For me a pistol is now a source of the most pleasurable thoughts.' Or 'This horrible and unremitting martyrdom has me thirst for the end and all portents suggest, the redemptive apoplexy is close at hand.' For a long time now he has lacked superlatives to express his sufferings; already they seem monotonous in their incessant and exasperating repetition, these wretched cries, which no longer have anything human about them, but which still ring out shrilly towards men, from the depths of this 'dog kennel existence'. Then suddenly flames – and one can only tremble before such a monstrous contradiction – in *Ecce Homo* that vigorous, proud, rigid confession of faith that appears to put the lie to every lament that preceded it: 'All in all, I have been (he speaks of the last fifteen years) in a state of quite excellent health.'

What then to believe? The thousand fold cries, or the lofty revelation? Both! Nietzsche's body was organically strong and capable of resistance. His inner trunk was broad and stable, supporting him like a tower, his roots were sunk deep in the soil of a long line of German parsons. All in all, '*summa summarum*', with regard to the plant, the organism, the fundamental nature of the spiritual body, Nietzsche was in truth a healthy man. Only his nerves were too delicate to withstand the violence and extreme sensations they endured and so they remained perpetually inflamed and were apt to revolt. (But a revolt that could never quite undermine his mind's steel grip on self-domination.) Nietzsche himself found the most charming image to paint that intermediary state between danger and security, when he speaks of 'the little fusillade' of his sufferings. Indeed, during this conflict, the inner walls of his life force are never breached. He exists like Gulliver in Lilliput, constantly assailed by the swarming little people of his sufferings. His nerves are always on the alert, he is continually on the lookout, keeping watch, his full attention monopolized by the debilitating and all-engrossing needs of self-defence. But never does a genuine illness manage to break him or render him vanquished (save perhaps for that unique sickness which for twenty years sunk mineshafts beneath the citadel of his spirit and then at a particular moment blew it into the air), for a monumental spirit like that of Nietzsche cannot be felled by a brief volley of shots, only an explosion can shatter the granite of such a mind. So, an enormous capacity for suffering opposes an enormous resistance to suffering, or rather an over-charged violence of feeling opposes an over-charged sensitive nerve in the motor system. For each nerve of the stomach, along with the heart and senses constituted for Nietzsche a highly accurate manometer, a delicate filigree-like instrument registering with tremendous amplitude the shifts and tension at the outbreak of the most painful stimulations. Nothing remained unconscious for his body (as for his mind). The most delicate fibre which in others stays muted, in him signals immediately with a quivering and a tearing and that 'raging irritability' shatters, into a thousand splinters, hazardous and piercing, his naturally energetic vitality. From this come the terrible cries, when at the slightest movement, with each sudden step of his life, he happens to touch one of these open twitching nerves.

This uncanny, almost demonic, hypersensitivity of Nietzsche's nerves, fugitive nuances that would never even cross the threshold of another's consciousness, and which undermined him so cruelly, is the sole root of his sufferings, but equally forms the primordial cell of his genial capacity for the appreciation of values. If his blood chances to register some physiological reaction, there does not have to be any tangible or affective cause: the atmosphere alone, with its meteorological adjustments hour by hour, is for him already the cause of infinite torments. Perhaps there has never existed a man of intellect so acutely sensitive to atmospheric conditions, so terrifyingly exposed to all the tensions and oscillations of meteorological phenomena, like a manometer, or mercury in the barometer: between his pulse and the atmospheric pressure, between his nerves and the degree of humidity, secret electrical contacts seem to exist; his nerves immediately register every metre of altitude, every change in pressure, in temperature, through a sense of discomfort in his organs, which react in accordance with each corresponding fluctuation in nature. Rain or an overcast sky depresses his vitality: 'A cloudy sky plunges me into a deep depression.' He feels in his very vitals the influence of a sky heavily charged with cloud; the rain reduces his 'potential', humidity weakens it, dry spells enliven it, the sun brings life, but winter is for him a kind of catalepsy and death. The quivering needle of his nerve barometer swings back and forth like an April temperature which never remains constant: what he must do then is to relocate himself within a cloudless landscape, upon the high plateau of the Engadine that no wind may disturb. And, just like the effect of the least change in cloud cover or pressure in the actual sky, his enflamed organs immediately sense the effect of all these pressure changes and atmospheric liberations upon the interior sky of the spirit. For each time a thought quivers in him, it shoots like a lightning fork across the strained knots of his nerves: the very act of thought is accomplished in Nietzsche's case, with passionate intoxication, with a rush of electricity so that it passes over his body like a storm and at each 'explosion of feeling, the mere blink of an eye is enough to modify the blood's circulation'. Body and mind in the most vital of all thinkers are so intimately linked to the atmosphere that for Nietzsche interior and exterior reactions are identical. 'I am neither body nor spirit, but rather a third element. I suffer everywhere and for everything.'

This singular disposition to discern so precisely the least stimulus was brutally exacerbated by the inactive incubating air of his life, through the fifteen years he spent in solitude. For three hundred and sixty five days of the year, no one else comes into physical contact with his own body, neither woman nor friend, for twenty-four hours of the day are spent in discourse with his own blood, pursuing a kind of uninterrupted dialogue with his nerves. Perpetually, at the centre of this tremendous silence, he rests on his palm the compass of his sensations and, in the manner of hermits, solitary men, bachelors and eccentrics; he observes in hypochondriac excess the slightest changes that occur in the function of his body. Others can forget because conversations and other day-to-day matters deflect their attention, as do games and general lassitude, or others may drown their feelings in wine and apathy. But Nietzsche, that genius for the diagnostic, continuously experiences the temptation to offer up himself for his own sufferings, seeking that curious pleasure of the psychologist choosing himself as subject, to be 'his own experiment and laboratory animal'. Again and again, with fine tweezers (at once surgeon and invalid), he dissects the suffering of his nerves and by doing so, like all natures overloaded with anxiety and imagination; he only serves to inflame his sensibility still further. Mistrusting the opinions of doctors, he takes on the role of his own doctor and 'medicates himself' through all stages of his life. He tries every conceivable method and cure, electric massages, dietary regimes, water therapies and medicinal baths; sometimes he blunts his excitability with bromide, then he stimulates it again with other potions. His meteorological like sensibility forces him to search unremittingly for a particular atmosphere, a location which could be for him 'the climate of his soul'. It might be Lugano, due to the lake air and an absence of wind, or Pfäfers and Sorrento; then he imagines the baths of Ragaz might deliver him from his malaise and that the health-giving area of St Moritz, the springs in the spa towns of Baden-Baden or Marienbad might afford him some well-being. For a whole Spring he finds the Engadine accords best with his own nature, with its 'invigorating and ozone rich air'; then it's a town of the south, Nice, with its 'dry' air, then Venice or Genoa. Now he wants to be in the forests, now he wants to be at the coast, now on the shore of a lake, now in quiet little towns 'with a simple and nourishing meal'. God knows how many thousands of kilometres this 'wandering fugitive' covers by rail, all to discover this fabled place where his nerves might be relieved of the burning and tearing and where his organs can cease being on permanent vigil. Little by little, he distills from his pathological experiences a kind of sanitary cartography for his own personal use, studying the great works of geology to discover the region that he seeks, like an Aladdin's ring, to finally master his body and bring peace to his soul. No journey is too long for him: Barcelona is in his sights and he dreams too of the high mountains of Mexico, of Argentina and even Japan. Geographic position, the dietary science of the climate and food gradually become second knowledge to him. At each location he notes the temperature, the air pressure; he measures to the millimetre, with a hydroscope and hydrostatic equipment, the atmospheric rainfall and ambient humidity, so much so that his body acts like a retort or the column of mercury in a thermo-meter. The same exaggeration is found in his dietary regime. There too, this 'recording' is to be found, a veritable medical tablature of precautions. The tea must be of a certain brand and served at a stipulated dosage so as to not do injury; a meat dish may be harmful, vegetables must be prepared in the correct manner. Little by little, this mania of medicalization, of diagnosing, becomes a pathological and egotistical trait, a tension, a hyper-awareness of the self. Nothing caused Nietzsche to suffer more than this eternal vivisection. As always, the psychologist suffers twice as much as anyone else, because he experiences the agony twice over: first in reality and then by observing himself.

But Nietzsche is a genius of violent opposites. In contrast to Goethe, who had a knack for knowing how to avoid danger, Nietzsche advances audaciously and takes the bull by the horns. The psychology, the spiritual effort – I have tried to show something of this – pushes the deeply impressionable man towards profound suffering and into the abyss of despair; but it is precisely the psychology, precisely the spirit which restore him to health. Like his sickness, Nietzsche's recovery comes only from the inspired knowledge he acquires of himself. Psychology, in a magic way, here becomes something therapeutic, a peerless application of that 'art of alchemy', which manages to 'extract value from something which has no value'. After ten years of relentless torment, he is 'at the lowest ebb of his vitality'; already they think him lost, ruined by his nerves, by an irremediable depression, given up to pessimistic self-abandonment. Then suddenly the spiritual attitude of Nietzsche takes an about-turn through one of those meteoric and inspired recoveries, both recognition and salvation of the self, that lend the history of the spirit such intensity and drama. Suddenly he draws from himself the very malady that saps his soul and presses it hard against his heart. Then comes the truly mysterious moment (whose date we cannot pinpoint precisely), one of those dazzling inspirations at the heart of his work, where Nietzsche 'discovers' his own sickness; where – surprised to find himself still breathing and to see that from the deepest depression, through the most grief-stricken periods of his existence, his productivity is growing – he proclaims with the most intimate conviction that his sufferings, his privations are merely a part, for him, 'of the cause', the sacred cause of his existence, the only cause that is sacred to him. At the hour when his mind has no more pity for his body and no longer participates in its trials, he sees his life for the first time with a new perspective and observes his sickness through a more profound intellect. With open arms, he knowingly accepts his destiny as a necessity, and as a fanatical 'advocate of life', he loves everything in his existence, even launching a hymn to his suffering in affirmation of Zarathustra, the jubilant 'Once more! Once more, for all eternity!' For him simple knowledge becomes a recognition and recognition a gratitude; for in this superior contemplation which lifts his gaze above his suffering and sees his own life only as a path to himself, he discovers (with that excessive joy conjured by the magic of extremes) that he owed all to his sickness and to no earthly power, that it was the mind tortures themselves that proved the greatest blessing: freedom, freedom of external existence, freedom of the spirit; for whenever he has risked settling down, delivered himself up to lassitude, released himself from the burden and abandoned his originality by becoming prematurely fossilized in some official post, a profession or a static spiritual form, it was the sickness that chased him out of it with its ruthless goad. It was the sickness that saved him from military service and returned him to science, that prevented him from being ossified in science and philology, that extricated him from the academic circles of Basel university, to enter 'retirement' and hence encounter the world, returning him as it were to his real self. He owed it to his afflicted eyes to have been 'liberated from the book', 'the greatest service I ever did myself'. Suffering tore him (painfully but helpfully) from all the husks that threatened to form around him, from all the relationships that began to enclose him. 'Sickness itself liberated me', he says of himself:

it was midwife to his inwardness and the sufferings it inflicted were not unlike those of childbirth. Thanks to it, life had become in his case, not a routine, but a renewal, a discovery: 'I discovered life, in some sense, like a novelty, myself included.'

For – and this is how the pained man now gratefully exalts his dolors in a grandiose hymn to the saint torment – only suffering leads to knowledge. Rude health is hollow and unsuspecting. It desires nothing and poses no questions and this is why there is no psychology among the healthy. All knowledge comes from suffering, 'pain always searches to know the causes, whilst pleasure remains in a fixed position and does not look backwards'. We become 'refined through pain'. Suffering, burrowing and scoring, breaks up the terrain of the soul and the tortuous labour of delving inwards, like the plough, turns the soil, enabling a new spiritual harvest. 'Mighty pain is the last liberator of the spirit; she alone forces us to descend into our ultimate depths', and he for whom it has been almost fatal has surely the right to proudly declaim these words: 'I know life better, because I have so often been at the point of losing it.'

It is not by artifice, by a negation, by palliatives and in idealizing his bodily distress that Nietzsche manages to surmount all these sufferings, but through the primitive force of his nature, through knowledge: the sovereign 'creator' of values discovers himself the true value of his illness. Martyr in reverse, he does not at first possess the faith to endure his torments; it is only from experiencing the torments themselves that he acquires this faith. But his knowledge chemistry not only discovers the value of sickness, but also its opposing pole: the value of health. Only their union can bear the accomplishment of life, that permanent tension of ordeal and ecstasy, thanks to which man rushes on into the infinite. Both are necessary: sickness, as the means, and health as the end; sickness as the path and health as the destination. For suffering, in Nietzsche's mind, is only the dark shore of sickness; the opposite shore is bathed in an inexpressible light: it is called recovery and only from the shore of suffering can it be reached. Now to heal, to recover one's health, signifies more than simply achieving a state of normal functioning life; it is not only a transformation, but something infinitely greater, an ascension, an elevation and a growth of perception: one emerges from sickness 'with a new skin, more sensitive, with a refined taste for pleasure, with a language more appreciative of all fine things, with a more joyful sensibility and a second more dangerous innocence at the heart of happiness', childlike and a hundred times more refined than formerly; and that second health following on the heels of illness, that health which is not blindly received, but is a treasure, sought out with great pain, bought with a hundred sighs and cries, this health 're-conquered with heavy losses' is a thousand times more vital than the cursory well-being of those who are always in fine fettle. Those who have tasted just once the quivering softness, the sparkling intoxication of this recovery, yearn always to experience the same sensation; to launch themselves again and again into the sulfurous fiery wave of burning torments, only in order to relocate that 'captivating sensation of health', that gilded drunkenness which, for Nietzsche, replaces and surpasses a thousand times over, all the vulgar stimulants of alcohol and nicotine. But hardly does Nietzsche perceive the meaning of sickness and enjoys the rapturous recovery, than he wants to make of it an apostolate through the sense of the world. Like all those in the grip of the demon, he is the slave of his own passions and is unable to draw back from that dazzling interplay between pleasure and pain. He desires that the torments martyrize him ever more intensely, so as to launch himself ever higher in the jubilant sphere of recovery, where all is clarity and vigour. In this shimmering and fervent drunkenness, he gradually confuses his vehement will for recovery with the thing itself, his fever with vitality and the vertigo of his downfall with an increase in power. Health! Health! This man so intoxicated with words brandishes them above him like a standard: it must be there the meaning of the universe, the purpose to life, the sole gauge of all values. And he who has for a dozen years groped in the shadows, from affliction to affliction, stifles his lament now in a hymn to life, the brute strength drunk on itself. With blazing colours, he unfurls the flag of the will to power, the will to live, the will to be hard and cruel and ecstatically presents this flag to coming humanity, not realizing that the strength which animates him and which allows him to raise his standard so high, is the same that will stretch the bow that sends the arrow which will kill him.

For Nietzsche, this final moment of health, which in exaltation rouses him to the dithyramb, is an autosuggestion, a 'contrived' health; precisely at the moment where he joyfully raises his hands to the heavens, in an outpouring of strength, vaunts (in *Ecce Homo*) his perfect health and swears that he has never been sick or decadent, already lightning quivers in his blood. What sings in him and triumphs, is not his life, but already his death, this is no longer the mind informed by science, but the demon snatching its victim. What he takes for light, for the red warmth of his blood conceals the fatal germ of his malaise, and what the clinical regard of each diagnosing doctor observes so clearly in this marvellous feeling of well-being enveloping him during those last hours, is what is commonly known as euphoria, that peculiar moment of bliss which heralds the end. Already the silver clarity which spreads over these last hours only projects before him the quivering sheen of another sphere, that of the demon, that of the beyond: but lost in his drunkenness he is no longer aware. He feels himself uniquely illuminated by all the splendour and gratitude of the earth. Ideas shoot out from him like flames; language trembles with a primordial power through all the pores of his discourse, and music suffuses his soul: everywhere he turns his gaze, he sees peace reign supreme. Ordinary people in the street smile at him. Each letter is a divine message and sparkling with happiness, he writes in a final letter to his friend Peter Gast: 'Sing me a new song. The world is transfigured and all the heavens rejoice.' It is from this transfigured sky that the fiery ray reaches him, confusing his beatitude and suffering into one indissoluble second. The two polarities of sentiment enter his swollen breast at the same moment and on his temples the veins throb with both life and death in a single apocalyptic music.

IV
The Don Juan of Knowledge

What matters is eternal vitality, not eternal life.

Immanuel Kant lived with knowledge like a coddling spouse; for forty years he lay alongside her in the same spiritual bed and with her procreated a whole line of German philosophic systems, whose descendants still inhabit our bourgeois world today. Their relationship with truth is always monogamous, like those of their spiritual sons: Schelling, Fichte, Hegel and Schopenhauer. What draws them towards philosophy is a desire for order, which has nothing of the demon about it, a strong German desire, objective and academic, tending to discipline the spirit and establish an orderly architecture of destiny. They possess a love of truth, a righteous love, durable, ever faithful. But this love is completely devoid of the erotic, of the flaming desire to consume oneself; they see in truth, in their truth, a wife and a possession from whom they will not be separated until the hour of their death and to whom they are never unfaithful. That is why there is always something in their relationship with truth which recalls a domestic setup; and in actual fact each of them built his own house only in order to shelter the marital bed and his betrothed, that is to say his possession, his philosophic system. And with masterful hand they labour, working with harrow and plough, this land which is theirs, this plot of the spirit which they conquered for humanity out of the primordial thicket of chaos. With prudence they ease back ever further the boundaries of their knowledge, secure at the heart of the culture of their time, and through diligence and sweat, they steadily increase the yield of the spiritual harvest.

But the passion for knowledge in Nietzsche is born from an altogether different temperament, from a virtually antipodal universe of the spirit. His stance before truth is wholly of the demonic kind; a hot breathed, nerve quivering, inquisitorial passion which never satisfies itself and is never exhausted, which never stops at any result and races on beyond all responses to further impatient and stubborn questioning. Never does he allow himself a knowledge set in stone, to which he could swear fidelity, to his wife, his 'system', his 'doctrine'. All stimulates him and nothing can hold him. As soon as a problem has relinquished its chaste state, the charm and the secret of modesty, he mercilessly abandons it to others without jealousy, just as Don Juan, his brother in instinct, does for his *mille e tre*, (one thousand and three) without caring about them again. For, in the same way that any great seducer seeks through all women, *the woman,* in the same way Nietzsche seeks, through all knowledge, *the knowledge* – the eternal knowledge that is insubstantial and never wholly accessible. What arouses him to the point of suffering and despair is not final conquest, not the actual pleasure of possession, but always uniquely the interrogation, the search and the hunt. His love is for incertitude not certitude, and as a result his sensual delight is 'turned towards the metaphysical' and consists of an '*amour plaisir*' for knowledge, a demonic desire to seduce, to expose, to passionately penetrate and violate each spiritual subject – echoing that of the Bible, in which man 'knows' woman and from so doing acquires her secret. He knows, this eternal relativist of values, that each of these acts of knowledge, each of these ardent possessions of the spirit is not 'definitive knowledge' and that truth, in the final sense of the word, does not allow itself to be possessed, for; 'he who thinks to be in possession of the truth, will never see how many things elude him!' That is why Nietzsche never sets up house, with a view to economizing and conserving, he builds no spiritual home; he wants (or perhaps he is forced by the nomadic instinct in his nature) to remain eternally without possessions, the solitary Nimrod who wanders with his weapons through all the forests of the spirit, who has no roof, no wife, no child, no servant, but who, on the other hand, has the thrill and pleasure of the hunt; like Don Juan, he adores not the enduring feeling but the fleeting 'moments of greatness and ecstasy'. He is solely attracted by an adventure of the spirit, by that 'dangerous perhaps' that stimulates and excites as long as the chase is on but as soon as attainment is reached loses its grip. He does not seek a quarry, but (as he describes himself in the Don Juan of knowledge) simply 'Spirit, stimulation, relish of the hunt and the intrigues of knowledge, as far as the highest and remotest stars, until there is nothing left to hunt but what is infinitely harmful in knowledge, like the drinker who ends up drinking absinthe and alcohol derived from acid.'

For the Don Juan, in Nietzsche's spirit, is not an epicurean, an extravagant savourer: in that he is unlike this aristocrat, this nobleman of refined tastes, with dull contentment of digestion, the indolent repose in satiety, the boastfulness that parades triumphs and replete satisfaction. The chaser of women – like the Nimrod of the spirit – is himself eternally stalked by an undying instinct; the seducer without scruples is himself seduced by a burning curiosity; the tempter always tempted to tempt women from their unsuspecting innocence, just as Nietzsche questions solely to question, for the unquenchable psychological pleasure to be savored. For Don Juan, the secret is in all and none, in all for a night and none for always: just as with the psychologist, in any given problem truth exists for only a single moment, never in perpetuity.

That is why the intellectual life of Nietzsche has no point of rest, lacks any mirror-like surface calm: it streams on, transforming, turning back on itself, consumed in rapid currents.

With other German philosophers, existence flows with epic tranquility; their philosophy seems to revolve comfortably and in some mechanical way, untangles a thread; they philosophize from deep in their armchairs, with limbs relaxed, and as they ponder, barely do they even register a raising of the blood pressure in their body, a fever in their destiny. Never with Kant does one have the forceful impression of a mind seized by thought as if by a vampire, painfully subjected to the terrifying necessity to create and elaborate ideas; and Schopenhauer, after his thirtieth year, following the achievement of *The World as Will and Idea*, wears the contented face of the employee about to collect his pension and retire amongst the thousand crumbs of bitterness left from a stagnant career. All proceed with precise and assured step along the path chosen by them, whilst Nietzsche always has the air of being hunted down and driven on towards the unknown. That is why the intellectual story of Nietzsche's life (like the adventures of Don Juan) always takes on dramatic form; it is a chain of alarming and hazardous episodes, a tragedy which, with no place to halt, in unrelenting movement, passes from one incident to another, ever more extreme, until the inevitable plummeting from on high and break up in the depths. And it is precisely this lack of respite during the search, this unceasing obligation to think, the demonic pressure to advance, that lends this unique existence such an unparalleled sense of tragedy and seductively transforms it into a work of art for us (for there is nothing in it of an academic or benignly bourgeois nature). Nietzsche was doomed, condemned to unremitting thought, like the wild hunter of legend condemned to hunt eternally; what was his pleasure became his torment, his affliction; and his breath, his diction, has that wild leaping, the heat and palpitations of a tracked prey; his soul has the ambition and raging thirst of one who can never rest and is never satisfied. That is why his laments of *Ahasverus*** resound so, like the cry that issues from him at the moment when he desires peace, pleasure, rest; but always the goad of eternal dissatisfaction bores violently down into his overextended soul: 'We love something but barely has this thing become a deep love, than the tyrant within us (that we might perhaps name our higher self) says: that must be sacrificed to me. And so we sacrifice it, but not without being tortured and roasted over a slow fire.' These Don Juan natures can never temper the heated passion for knowledge, never savour the loving embrace of woman, for the demon of dissatisfaction has them by the scruff of the neck and pushes them on ever further (this same demon which pursued Hölderlin and Kleist and all the other fanatical idolaters of the infinite). And it's like the howl of a prey in flight pierced by an arrow, when Nietzsche, pursued by the demon of knowledge, cries out 'They are everywhere, the gardens of Armida, thus there must always be a new tearing free and fresh bitterness in the heart. I must raise my foot, my weary and wounded foot, and because I am obliged to do so, I often cast behind me a joyless backward glance towards the beautiful things which could no longer hold me – precisely because they could no longer hold me!'

Such cries from deep within, such indomitable groans issuing from the innermost recesses of suffering, are absent in all else that employs the term philosophy. Perhaps an equable fervour burst forth from the mystics of the Middle Ages, the heretics, the saints of the Gothic age (albeit in more muted manner and with

---

* Ahasverus is the name given to the 'wandering Jew', the character who appears in the legend of Ahasverus as he who was supposed to have taunted Christ on his way to the crucifixion and was thus condemned to roam the earth forever. The legend appears to have originated in Eastern Europe during the middle ages. It was celebrated alongside the cult of the vampire in the Romantic period and Shelley casts Ahasverus as a lead promethean figure in his poem 'Queen Mab'.

clenched teeth) through a darkly cloaked language. Pascal, who plunged his whole soul into the purgatory of doubt, he too knew this upheaval, this devastation of the ever-questing soul, but never, not with Leibniz, nor Kant, Hegel or Schopenhauer were we shaken by such an elemental tone. For, as loyal as these scientific natures may be, as courageous and resolute as their concentration towards everything might seem to us now, they cannot launch themselves with all their being, undivided, heart and entrails, nerves and flesh, with all their destiny, into the heroic game of knowledge. They burn like a candle, that is to say from the top down, from the head, the mind. A part of their existence, the temporal part, private and hence also the most personal, always remains sheltered from fate, whilst Nietzsche risks himself totally, he who continually approaches peril 'not only with the antennae of icy thought', but with all the ecstasies and torments of his blood, with all the impetus of his destiny. His thoughts do not only come from beyond, from destiny itself, but are the feverish product of a stimulated hunted blood, of nerves quivering with violence, of senses never sated, of the total embrace of vital feeling: this is why his ideas, like those of Pascal, extend tragically, in an impassioned story of the soul; they are the consequence, pushed to the extreme, of the most perilous well-nigh fatal adventures – a living drama that strikes us to the core (whilst the life stories of other philosophers fail to budge the intellectual horizon an inch). And yet, even in the most bitter distress, he would not want to exchange his life, his 'hazardous life', with theirs, which is a model of order, for what the rest seek in knowledge, an *aequitas animae**, a stable repose for the soul, a battlement to repel an excess of feelings, Nietzsche despises because it diminishes the vital impulse. In his eyes, for the tragic figure, the heroic one, there is in the 'miserable struggle for

---

* Latin concept of justice, fairness, equality or symmetry.

existence', no increase of security, no protection against emotional turbulence. No security, and never any satisfaction or contentment with what one has! 'How can you be thrown into this marvellous incertitude and multiplicity of existence without questioning it, without trembling with the desire and passion that is the result of such questioning!' says he, disdainfully mocking those who stay put by the fire, the easily contented. How dull they seem in their cold certitudes, snugly embalmed in the shell of their systems; what attracts him is always the dangerous wave, adventure, seductive multiplicity, glittering enticement, eternal rapture and eternal disillusion. How they continue to practise their philosophy in the warm dwelling place of their systems, how they go about it like commerce, augmenting their possessions righteously; no, he is only attracted by the game, by the stakes of higher riches, that of his own existence. For, adventurer that he is, he lacks even the desire to possess his own life: here too, he still craves heroic excess: 'It is eternal vitality that counts, not eternal life.'

With Nietzsche there appears for the first time upon the high seas of German philosophy the black flag of a pirate ship: a man of a different type, another race, a new brand of heroism, a philosophy no longer clad in professorial and scholarly robes, but armed and armoured for the struggle. Others before him, comparably bold and heroic navigators of the spirit, had discovered continents and empires; but with only a civilizing and utilitarian interest, in order to conquer them for humanity, in order to fill in the philosophic map, penetrating deeper into the *terra incognita* of thought. They plant the flag of God or of the spirit on the newly conquered lands, they construct cities, temples and new roads in the novelty of the unknown and on their heels come the governors and administrators, to work the acquired terrain and harvest from it the commentators and teachers, men of culture. But the final objective of their labours, is rest, peace and stability: they want to increase the possessions of the world, propagate norms and laws, establish a superior order. Nietzsche, in contrast, storms into German philosophy like the filibusters making their entrance into the Spanish empire at the end of the sixteenth century, a wild unruly swashbuckling swarm of desperados, without nation, ruler, king, flag, home or residence. Like them he conquers nothing for himself, or anyone following him, not for a god, or a king, or a faith, but uniquely for the pleasure of conquest, for he wants to acquire, conquer and possess nothing. He concludes no treaty nor builds a house, he scorns the rules of war put in place by philosophers and he seeks no disciple; he, the zealous troublemaker of all 'brown rest', of all comfortable establishment, only seeks to pillage, to destroy the order of ownership, the assured and appreciative peace of men; to propagate by fire and sword that ever awakening vitality of the spirit, which is as precious to him as their dreary and barren peace. He emerges audaciously, sacks the fortresses of morals, tramples the fences of laws, he gives no quarter to any man and no excommunication from church or crown can hold him. In his wake, as with the incursion of the filibusters, stand desecrated churches, profaned thousand-year-old shrines, crumbled altars, humiliated sentiments, crushed convictions, the cradle of morals plundered, the horizon ablaze, a beacon of brazenness and power. And he never returns, to enjoy what he has acquired, to make it his property: only the unknown, that which has never been fully conquered or properly explored, this is his eternal domain, his only pleasure is to exercise force, to 'rouse the sleepers'. Jettisoning all beliefs, swearing no oath to a homeland and having fastened the black flag of the immoralist to his masthead, he stands before the sacred unknown, the infinite solitude to which he is demonically fraternal, and across which he makes fresh and ever more perilous crossings. Sword in fist, his foot on the powder barrel, he steers his vessel away from the shore. Alone before all dangers he sings to himself, to glorify himself, his buccaneer song, his song of flame, his hymn of destiny.

Yes, I know from where I came,
Never sated like the flame
I glow and consume myself,
All I catch becomes light,
Carbon is all that I leave,
Yes assuredly I am flame– .

V
The Passion of Sincerity

For you there is but one commandment: be pure.

Early on, Nietzsche had proposed to write a book called *Passio nuova* or 'The Passion of Sincerity'. He never actually wrote this book, but far better he lived it. For a fanatical and fervent sincerity, a love of exalted truth, the high tension of torment forms the primordial cell in Nietzsche's growth and metamorphosis: it sits, deeply rooted, snagged in the flesh, the nerves and the brain, the coiled spring of the superman, maintaining his thought in constant tension, lifting it with mortal strength towards all the difficulties of life.

Sincerity, integrity, purity! It seems surprising to hear from the 'immoralist' Nietzsche no peculiar and primitive instinct, nothing outside of what the bourgeois, the grocer, the shopkeeper and the lawyer declares with equal pride, their virtue: honesty, sincerity until the grave, an intellectualized virtue akin to ordinary folk's mediocre and conventional sentiments. But in such a sentiment intensity is all and not contentment; and it is for those natures in the grip of the demon to reappraise the notion of sincerity for so long rendered rhetorical and banal and transport it into creative chaos, into a sphere of infinite tension. They infuse with the elements, even the most insignificant and worn away by convention, the colours of fire and the ecstasies of glorification. A being in thrall to the demon always transforms chaotically and is filled with untamed strength. This is why the sincerity of Nietzsche has nothing to do with the bloodless honesty of ordinary men; his love for truth is wholly a flame, a demon of truth, a demon of lucidity, a feral savage in quest of plunder and always on the hunt, gifted with the most subtle faculty of smell and the barbarous instincts of the carnivorous beast. A sincerity like that of Nietzsche has nothing in common with the measured prudence of shopkeepers, nor with that brutal and unwieldy 'Michael Kohlhaas'* brand of sincerity common to a number of thinkers (Luther, for example), who wearing blinkers and seeing neither to left nor right, precipitate themselves furiously down the path of a single truth, their own. For as violent and coarse as the passion in Nietzsche's truth seeking might often be, it is always too highly strung, too cultivated to ever become narrow: never does it resort to obstinacy or stubbornness, but ranges from problem to problem, quivering like a flame, consuming and illuminating each and is never detained by one alone. This duality is magnificent. With Nietzsche passion and sincerity are always effectively maintained. Perhaps never before has so great a psychological genius possessed at the same time such a high degree of ethical stability and character.

This is why Nietzsche is predestined more than any other to think lucidly: he who understands and practises philosophy with a passion leaves himself open to all his being with that sense of rapture known only to those who have achieved perfection. One savours this sincerity in him like music, this veracity, this bourgeois virtue (I have said this already) that normally is considered only objectively, as a necessary ferment in the life of the spirit. The splendid exaltations, the crescendo in counterpoint that exists in his love of truth are like a magisterial fugue of the intellect, passing like the movements of a storm from a virile andante to a splendid *maestoso*† – perpetually renewing themselves in astonishing polyphony. Lucidity here becomes

---

* Novella of 1811 written by Heinrich von Kleist based on a sixteenth-century story of Hans Kohlhase. (The style in the form of a chronicle seemed modern for its time; this and the theme of a fanatical quest for justice resonated with later writers.)

† Musical instruction; in a majestic and stately manner.

something supernatural. This man, half blind, groping painfully about before him and dwelling owl-like in the shadows, possessed, in psychological terms, the gaze of a falcon, a gaze that can, like any bird of prey, race in a split second from the loftiest heights of his thought to rest on the faintest tracks, upon the most speculative and inconstant nuances, with infallibility. Before this awesome intellect, this unrivalled psychological probing, nothing can evade attention or remain hidden: his X-ray eye pierces through garments, hair, skin and flesh, to the innermost depths of a problem. And just as his nerves react to the pressure of the atmosphere with barometric precision, his intellect, blessed with an equally fine instrument, records via the nerves, with the same impeccable reaction, every nuance of moral consideration. But Nietzsche's psychology does not issue solely from an intelligence hard and clear as a diamond, but issues from the body itself and derives from that extraordinary sensitivity towards values by which he tastes and smells all that is not fresh or pure in the human sphere, accepting this as a natural function: 'My genius resides in my nostrils.' 'An extreme faithfulness towards everything' is for him not a moral dogma, but a primary condition, elementary and essential to existence: 'I perish when I am in an unclean environment.' Absence of clarity and moral feculence depress and agitate him, like lowering clouds, diminish the fountainhead of his nerves and like a fatty or undercooked dish aggravates his stomach: his body rebels in advance of his spirit. 'I possess a most unpleasant irritability as regards the instinct of purity, so much so that I perceive physiologically, I actually feel in the most intimate sense the proximity and depth of the souls entrails.' He sniffs out with unerring certitude all that has been infected with morality, through the incense of churches, artificial untruths, patriotic slogans or any other narcotic of consciousness; he has a fine sense of smell for all that is rotten, corrupted and unhealthy, to nose out the lingering odour of intellectual poverty that resides in the mind; lucidity, purity, cleanliness are the necessary conditions for his intellect, but also his body (as I suggested earlier), requires pure air and clear sharp contours: psychology is as he himself suggests, 'an interpretation of the body', the prolongation of a nervous disposition into the domain of the mind. Against Nietzsche's sacred sensibility, all other psychologists appear somewhat leaden and heavy-handed. Even Stendhal, who was blessed with nerves of extreme delicacy, cannot match him, because he lacks the passionate insistence, the vigorous movement: he is content to idly note his observations, whilst Nietzsche throws himself with all the ardour of his being into the least problem of knowledge, like the bird of prey plunging from on high towards the most insignificant crawling animal. Dostoyevsky alone possessed nerves of a comparable clarity (likewise assailed by hypertension, and afflicted by a morbidly unhealthy sensibility). But Dostoyevsky is inferior to Nietzsche in terms of veracity. He can be unjust; he can exaggerate, right in the midst of his enquiry, whilst Nietzsche, even in his most profound rapture, never sacrifices a crumb of his faithfulness. That is why perhaps never before has anyone been so predestined by nature and birth to be a psychologist; never has a spirit been so perfectly formed to become the subtle barometer of the souls meteorology; never has the study of values possessed such a precise and sublime instrument. But it is not enough in the most adept psychologist to wield only the sharpest scalpel with the best cutting edge, he must also have a grip of steel, a supple and durable metal, it must not waver or be withdrawn during the psychological operation, for such an operation demands more than talent alone, it demands character and the courage to 'think all that one knows'. In the ideal case, like that of Nietzsche, it is a faculty of knowing fused with a virile and primitive force of the will to know. The genuine psychologist must will to see what is before him with as much strength as he possesses, he must look neither left nor right, sentimental indulgences, personal fears and anxieties must not deter him from this path; he must not let himself wander off through scruples or feelings. With the dedicated thinkers and guardians 'whose labour is vigilance', there is no room for a spirit of conciliation, of bonhomie, reserve or compassion, no room for the weaknesses (or virtues) of the bourgeois, conventional man. It is not permitted to these warriors, these conquerors of the spirit to voluntarily allow a truth to slip away which they seized on one of their audacious patrols. In the domain of knowledge, 'blindness is not a fault, but a cowardice' and a good nature is a crime, for he who fears the shame or fear of doing someone down, he who cannot bear the accusative cries of those he has unmasked or to observe the ugliness of their nakedness, can never hope to discover the supreme secret. Any truth not pushed to the furthest extremity, any veracity not of the absolute, has no ethical value. From this comes that hardness Nietzsche reserves for those who, through idleness or cowardice of thought, neglect the sacred work of resolution. From this comes his fury with Kant, for having re-introduced to his system of values, via the back door and with averted eye, the concept of a divinity; hence his hatred for all those in philosophy who keep their eyelids firmly shut, his hatred for the 'devil or demon of nebulosity' who veils or cravenly obscures supreme knowledge. There are no truths on the grand scale which can be achieved through flattery; there are no secrets which might be garnered from the usual seductive prattle: it is only through violence, through strength and inflexibility that nature will relinquish what is most precious to her; only through brute strength can a moral 'on the grand scale' affirm 'the atrocity and majesty of infinite claims'. All that is concealed demands a durable grip, implacable intransigence: without sincerity there is no knowledge; without resolution there is no sincerity, or 'consciousness of the spirit'. 'Where my sincerity disappears I am blind; where I desire to know, I also desire to be sincere, that is to say hard, severe, narrow, cruel and inexorable.'

As with his falcon's gaze, this destiny of radicalism, this hardness and implacability was not handed to Nietzsche's psychology on a plate: he rather paid for them with his whole life, his rest, his sleep, his well-being. From an originally gentle, somewhat carefree, accessible and always well-disposed temperament, Nietzsche was obliged to resort to a wholly Spartan will, to make himself inaccessible and uncompromising with regard to his own feelings: he spent half his life, it could be said, in the inferno. He had to look deep inside himself to understand the painful character of this moral process. For at the same time as his 'weakness', his gentleness and goodness, Nietzsche also puts to the torch everything that unites men: he loses friendships, relationships, all ties; and his last scrap of life becomes little by little so febrile, so red hot by its own flame that all those who seek to touch it burn their hand. Just as the infernal stone to expunge impurities cauterizes the wound, Nietzsche ruthlessly burns his feelings, to render himself pure and sincere. He brands himself unceremoniously with the red-hot iron of total truthfulness: which is why his solitude is also the result of constraint. But with true fanaticism he sacrifices all he loves, even Richard Wagner, whose friendship once represented the most sacred of encounters; he makes himself poor, solitary and despised. He prefers to become a miserable hermit in order to stay true and to carry out to the very end the mission of his integrity. Like all those possessed by the demon, his passion, in his case, probity, becomes progressively dominant, monomaniac, and consumes in its flames all other areas of his life; and like all those possessed by the demon, by the end he knew nothing more than his passion. This is why we must throw out once and for all these schoolmaster-type questions of 'What was Nietzsche look-ing for?' 'What did Nietzsche think?' 'Towards which system, which philosophy did he tend?' Nietzsche wanted nothing. There was simply within him an excessive passion for truth, a passion that celebrated itself. It knew no finality. Nietzsche did not employ thought to improve or instruct the universe, nor to satisfy it or himself: his ecstatic intoxication with thought is the end in itself, a pleasure quite satisfied with itself, an eminently personal and individual state of ecstasy, entirely egoist and ele-mentary, like any demonic possession. Never in this colossal spending of strength, does he speak of a 'doctrine' (it was long ago he overtook 'the noble childishness and beginnings of dog-matism') and still less of a religion: 'In me there is nothing of the founder of religion. Religions are for the bloodless herd.' Nietzsche practised philosophy like art, and like the artist he did not search for results, something in cold definition, but a style: 'the great style of morality', and like the artist he experiences all those quiverings of sudden inspiration (and he savoured them). This is perhaps why labelling Nietzsche a philosopher in the first place is a mistake, that is to say a friend of Sophia, of wis-dom. For the passionate man always lacks wisdom and nothing was more foreign to Nietzsche than to merely proceed towards the habitual objective of philosophers, to an equilibrium of feel-ing, to repose in a *tranquillitas*, a sated 'brown' wisdom at the rigid point of a unique conviction. He 'spends and consumes' successive convictions; rejecting what he has acquired and for this reason we would do better to call him Philaleth, a fervent lover of Aletheia, truth, that chaste and cruelly seducing god-dess, who unceasingly, like Artemis, lures her lovers into an eternal hunt only to remain ever inaccessible behind her tattered veils. Truth with Nietzsche cannot be understood as a crys-talline rigid form, but rather the brazen volition to be true and remain true, not the ultimate term of the equation, but an unceasing demonic elevation to a higher level, to a tension of one's own most vital feeling, an exaltation of life in its most achieved consummation. Nietzsche had no desire to find happiness but only to be true. He did not seek rest (like nine-tenths of philosophers), but rather in the position of slave and server of the demon, the final superlative to express all excitations and all movements. Every struggle for the inaccessible acquires the character of heroism and all heroism must end in that most sacramental of all consequences: downfall.

Inevitably this virtual fanaticism for integrity, so dangerous and unrelenting, leads Nietzsche into a murderous and suicidal conflict with the world. Nature, which is made up of a thousand disparate elements, naturally rejects any unilateral element. All life is fundamentally built on conciliation, on tolerance (this is what Goethe, he who reflected so wisely the essence of nature in his being, recognized and applied to himself from an early stage). To maintain itself in balance, nature needs, like man, to occupy the middle ground, concessions, compromise and the forming of pacts. And he who has the fortitude to take an anti-natural and anthropomorphic stance and not adhere to the superficiality, the concessions and conciliations of this world, he who wants to wrench himself free from the network of liaisons and conventions woven over millennia, places himself in mortal opposition to society and nature. The more an individual earnestly attempts to 'breath absolute purity', the more he becomes a victim of his epoch. The more he persists, like Hölderlin, in the desire to give uniquely poetic form to an essentially prosaic life, the more he attempts, like Nietzsche, to penetrate the earthly nexus, 'pure thought', the more the heroic revolt against customs and rules drives the risk taker into irremediable solitude, into a magnificent losing battle. It is what Nietzsche terms 'tragic sentiments', the resolution to go as far as it takes in any given feeling passes from the spirit into living reality and creates tragedy. He who seeks to impose on his life but one law, he who in the chaos of passions wants to culminate in a single passion – his own – becomes solitary and to such an extent that he is destroyed – a foolhardy dreamer if his actions are unconscious, but a hero if he is aware of the danger but nevertheless goes forward to meet it. Nietzsche, so impassioned in his sincerity, is one who remains conscious. He knows full well the danger to which he has exposed himself. He knows from the first moment, from the very earliest writings that his thought turns around a dangerous and tragic spindle, that he lives a precarious life, but (like so many heroes of the spirit with a truly tragic character) he only loves life because of this danger, which devastates his own life. 'Build your homes by Vesuvius!' he cries to the philosophers, to spur them on to a higher consciousness of destiny, for 'the degree of danger in which a man lives with himself' is for him the only measure of greatness worthy of the name. Only he who stakes everything on one hand can access the infinite; only he who risks his own life can give to his narrow terrestrial form the measure of the infinite. *Fiat veritas, pereat vita**, what matter if it costs him his life, if he advances truth. Passion has a higher value than existence; the sense of life is worth more than life itself. With immense power, Nietzsche gives epic form to this thought, which overtakes his own destiny: 'We all prefer the destruction of humanity to the destruction of knowledge.' The more his fate becomes insecure, the more he is aware of the lightning fork suspended above his head in the always purer skies of the spirit, the more the hunger for this conflict sends him into jubilant fatalism. 'I know my fate,' he says on the eve of his collapse, 'one day my name will be associated with something extraordinary, a crisis unlike any on earth. The memory of the most profound collision of conscience, a decision against all that

* 'Let truth be done, and let life perish.'

was until that moment held sacred and inviolable.' But Nietzsche cherishes this ultimate abyss of all knowledge and his whole being advances with this lethal resolution. 'How much truth can man take?' Such was the question this courageous thinker posed across his entire existence; for to properly measure the true depths of man's capacity for knowledge, one must breach the security zone and scale the ladder where one is no longer supported, where the final knowledge is deadly, where the light is too close and blinding. It is precisely these final few advancing paces which are the most unforgettable and powerful in the tragedy of his fate: never was his spirit more illuminated, his soul more impassioned, his words brimming with more jubilation and music than when he launches himself, in full consciousness and with his entire will, from the uplands of his life into the abyss of annihilation.

VI
Transfiguration Towards the Self

The snake which cannot shed its skin, perishes.
Likewise those spirits which are unable to change
their concepts are no longer spirits.

Men of order, as blind as they may be before all that is original, possess an unfailing instinct for what is hostile to them; long before Nietzsche revealed himself to be an immoralist and the fire-raiser of their narrow enclosure of morals, they sensed in him an enemy: they had the measure of him before he did himself. He discomfited them, (no one mastered better than he 'the gentle art of making enemies') as the doubter type, the eternal outsider in all categories, the mongrel philosopher, philologist, revolutionary, artist, literary figure and musician – from the very first hour the specialists had despised him for his crossing of boundaries. Barely had the young philologist published his first work on the subject than the master of philology Wilamowitz (who stayed anchored to his academic position for half a century, whereas his charge proceeded to immortality) nailed him to the yardarm in front of all his colleagues for daring to exceed professional limits. The Wagnerians mistrusted him – and how justifiably! – for his impassioned panegyrics towards the master, the philosophers for his knowledge: even before he had emerged from the chrysalis of philology, even before his wings had formed, Nietzsche already had the experts ranged against him. Only Richard Wagner, genius and agent of change, cherishes this evolving spirit, this future enemy. But the rest sniff the air and sense a danger in his risqué manner and penchant for extremes. They sense a man who is wavering, unfaithful to his convictions, lost in that freedom without brakes that the most liberated of men practise towards all things and hence to their own self. And even to this very day his authority intimidates and makes them reticent, these specialists who would so much like to enclose 'the lawless prince' in a system, a doctrine, a religion or a message. They would like him to be like them, rooted in convictions, walled up in a conception of the universe, all that he dreads most. They would like to impose on this defenseless man a definitive position without contradiction, and place this nomad (he who conquered the infinite world of the spirit) in a temple, a dwelling place, he who never had such a shelter nor desired one.

But Nietzsche could not be caged in a doctrine, nor rooted in a conviction, and never in these pages has it been the intention to extract, in scholarly fashion, from one of the most moving tragedies of the mind, a cold 'theory of knowledge', for never did this fervent relativist of all values experience a prolonged attachment to any word that departed his lips, to any conviction of his conscience, to any passion in his soul and never did he feel bound by them. 'A philosopher uses and consumes convictions,' he responds haughtily to those sedentary spirits who proudly extol their character and their doctrine. Each of his opinions is only a transition; and even his own self, his skin, his body, his intellectual structure, were in his eyes, only a multiplicity, 'a meeting house for many souls': one day he made, quite literally, the most audacious of all declarations. 'It is disadvantageous for the thinker to be linked to any single person. When a man finds himself, it is preferable that he loses himself again from time to time and then rediscovers himself once more.' His essence is one of perpetual transformation, knowledge of himself through loss of himself, that is to say a continual becoming and eschewing of any rigid composed state: that's why the only imperative in life encountered in his writings is 'become what you are'. Goethe said it too, that when he was at Jena they were always looking for him in Weimar, and Nietzsche's image of the shedding of a snake skin, can in fact be traced back a century before to a letter by Goethe, but what contrasts between the deliberate reflective evolution of Goethe and the eruptive metamorphosis of Nietzsche! For Goethe extends his life from a fixed point, just as a tree adds each year another ring to its internal hidden trunk; and as he sheds his exterior bark, he becomes firmer, stronger, higher and sees ever further. His development is down to patience, a tenacious and continuing force of absorption, able at one and the same time to encourage growth and consolidate resistance in a complete defence of the self, whilst Nietzsche knows only violence, the turbid ferociousness of his will. Goethe expands himself without ever sacrificing a part of himself; he never needs to withdraw into himself to raise himself. Nietzsche on the other hand, the man of transformation, is always obliged to destroy himself in order to reconstruct himself anew. All his self isolation and fresh discoveries are the result of a murderous savaging of the self and the sacrifice of beliefs, decompensation; to go ever higher he is forced to jettison a part of his self, (whereas Goethe sacrifices nothing and is content to chemically transfigure and distill his elements). To reach an ever more open and higher viewing position, Nietzsche must always pass through the maw of pain and mutilation: 'The rupture of all individual bonds is hard, but a wing grows in place of each bond.' Being of a fundamentally demonic nature, he knows only the most brutal of transformations, as through a combustion process: like the phoenix that is consumed in fire, to be reborn with new colours and fresh vigour, singing, hovering over its own ash, thus the intellectual spirit of his soul must pass through the funeral pyre of contradiction, so that the spirit rises again ever renewed and liberated from convictions past their prime.

In his ever-changing view of the universe, nothing remains intact, nothing can resist contradiction: this is why his diverse phases never follow each other in an atmosphere of fraternity, but with hostility. He is always setting out on the road to Damascus; not once does he change his belief or sentiment, but countless times, for with him each new spiritual element penetrates not only the mind, but right to the very guts: moral and intellectual knowledge transforming in him govern the circulation of his blood, his feeling and his thought. Like a reckless gambler, Nietzsche (Just as Hölderlin had postulated) 'exposed the whole soul to the destructive power of reality). And right from the start, the experience and impressions he experiences take the form of violent and volcanic eruptions. When as a young student in Leipzig he reads Schopenhauer's *The World as Will and Idea,* he is unable to sleep for ten days; his whole being is thrown into chaos as by a cyclone; the faith on which he had leant, simply collapsed in ruins; and when his bedazzled mind gradually recovered from this frenzy, he stood before a new world view and a new ideology. His encounter with Richard Wagner becomes the source of an impassioned love, which infinitely extends the range of his sensibility. When he returns to Triebschen from Basel, his life possesses a whole new meaning; from one day to the next the philologist is no more and a perspective on the past, of history, gives way to that of the future. And it is precisely because his soul is so anchored in spiritual apotheosis that the ensuing rupture with Wagner leaves such a gaping wound, one which proves almost fatal, a wound that suppurates and weeps, a wound that will never properly heal. Always, with a shuddering of the earth, at each of these spiritual shock waves, the whole edifice of his convictions caves in and Nietzsche is yet again obliged to reconstruct from top to bottom. Nothing grows in him gently, silently, organically, like those elements of nature, never does his interior life extend through undisclosed labour, widening its base: everything, even his own ideas – strike him 'like lightning bolts'; always a universe must be laid ruin within him so that the new cosmos may arise. This explosive force of Nietzsche is unparalleled. 'I would like, he writes one day, to be liberated from the expansions of feeling that leave in their wake these happenings. It has not been lost on me that one day I will perish from such an event.' And, in fact there is something that perishes in him in the vortex of these spiritual rebirths; for in his internal fibres, something tears, as if a steel blade were slicing through all former relations. Always the spiritual dwelling place is put to the torch, inciner-ated, left unrecognizable by the flame jet of fresh inspiration. With Nietzsche, there is in all these transformations both the convulsion of death and of birth. Never before has a human being developed through such horrifying torments, never before has a man lost so much blood in seeking his inner self. This is why his books are, so to speak, clinical case studies of these operations, methods employed in vivisection, a sort of obstetric of the free spirit. 'My books only deal with victories over my-self.' They are the histories of his transformations, of his preg-nancy and birth, of his death and resurrections, the history of wars he has waged against his own self, tortures and executions he has inflicted on himself, and in total, a biography of all the beings Nietzsche was and is becoming over the two decades of his spiritual existence.

What seems incontestably characteristic in these perpetual transformations is the presence of a regressive movement. Take Goethe (he is always the one we find before us, the most sym-bolic of all human types) as the prototype of an organic nature which always finds itself uncannily in accord with each step of the universe; the stages of his own development are symbolic-ally reflected in the stages of life. In his youth Goethe possesses a fiery enthusiasm, in middle age a meditative quality and in old age the most lucid thought: the rhythm of his mind corresponds organically to the temperature of his blood. His chaos is found at the beginning (as with any young man); a sense of order is found at the close of his career (as with any elderly man); he becomes conservative having once been revolutionary, a man of science having once dabbled in the occult, a mind judiciously ordered, where once it had been extravagant.

Nietzsche is the polar opposite to Goethe. Instead of aspiring to a greater integration of his self, he willed an ever more passionate disintegration: like all those gripped by the demon, he becomes ever more overheated, more impatient, more vehement, more revolutionary, more chaotic as he advances in age. Already his exterior attitude is at odds with a conventional evolution. Nietzsche sets out from old age. At only twenty-four years old, when his friends are given up to the ribald life of students, drinking beer, carousing and indulging in horseplay, Nietzsche is already a professor, holding chair of philology at the prestigious university of Basel. His real friends are men of closer to fifty or sixty years, hoary thinkers like Jacob Burckhardt and Ritschl, and his closest companion is the leading artist of his age, the solemn Richard Wagner. Grim determination, brazen sternness, unswerving objectivity, make of him a learned man rather than an artist and in his books is heard the superior and pedagogic tone of a seasoned campaigner. He strongly suppresses his poetic energies, the updraught of music. Like some old fossilized privy councillor he sits hunched over his manuscripts, drawing up his indexes, content to revise dusty pandects (a collection of ancient roman judicial verdicts, once commonly the bedrock of German law). Nietzsche's gaze at the beginning is completely turned towards 'history', to what is dead and had once been. The pleasures of his life are walled in by a kind of 'old man monomania'; his happiness and high spirits are masked by professorial dignity and his eyes never leave his books and scholarly problems. At age twenty-seven, *The Birth of Tragedy* appears as the first covert breakthrough into the present: but the author of this book is, in spiritual terms, still wearing the mask of the philologist and if there is in this work a first flame of the fire to come, the herald-ing glimmer of a love for the present, of a passion for art, they remain below the surface. At around thirty, the age when the conventional man turns to a bourgeois existence, at the time when Goethe became a state councilor, when Kant or Schiller took up professorships, Nietzsche had already left his official functions behind him and abandoned with great relief his chair at Basel. It is then he takes the first step towards his true self; the first movement to enter his own universe, his first inward metamorphosis and this rift also constitutes his awakening as an artist. The real Nietzsche begins with his incursion into the pres-ent, the tragic Nietzsche, the man out of time, whose gaze is now turned to the future and whose heart yearns for the new man who may one day emerge. In between he lays the firedamp of transformations, consummate eversions of his inner self – the abrupt wind change from philology to music, from gravity to ecstasy, from sober forbearance to the dance. At thirty-six Nietzsche is the outlaw prince, immoralist, sceptic, poet and musician, a 'better youth' than he had ever been in younger days, free of the past and of all scholarship, he resists the claims of the present, and pledges himself to the men of the future. Unlike the conventional artist where the years of development lead to a sense of stability, evolving into a more sober-minded and methodical existence, in Nietzsche they only serve to liber-ate him from all attachments. The rhythm of this rejuvenation is diabolical and without parallel. At forty the language of Nietz-sche, his thought and being contain more red blood cells, exhibit a far healthier hue, display more temerity, passion and music than as a youth of seventeen and the solitary of Sils-Maria fairly glides through his work as if on wings, like a dancer, with much lighter step than the prematurely aged professor of twenty-four. In Nietzsche there is an intensification of life rather than a slow-ing down: his transformations become ever swifter, freer, more airborne, multifaceted, resilient, tense, malicious, cynical; he finds no 'standpoint' anywhere for a mind in perpetual motion. Barely has he anchored somewhere, than 'his skin chaps and splits'; in the end his own life is incapable of following the metamorphosis of his spirit and the changes in him gradually take on a cinematographic like tempo, where the image continually quivers and shifts. Those who think themselves closest to him, those friends of periods in his life now passed, almost all of whom are rooted in their scholarship, their conviction, their system are ever more alarmed at each new encounter. With horror they discover a rejuvenated intellect, new features bearing no relation to former ones; and always on the path to transfiguration, Nietzsche seems to be stood as if before a phantom when he hears his own title pronounced, when they 'confuse' him with this 'Professor Friedrich Nietzsche of Basel', the philologist, that barely remembered wise old sage he had once been twenty years earlier. Perhaps no one has ever hurled a former life so far away from himself as Nietzsche, brushing aside all rudiments and feelings of another time: then comes the horrifying solitude of his final years. For he has severed all ties with the past; and the rhythm of his last years, his last metamorphosis, is too frenzied to permit new relationships to form. He streaks past all men and all phenomena and the more he comes closer, or appears to come closer to the self, the more feverish the craving to escape from himself becomes. Ever more radical are the modifications to his being, ever more sudden are the leaps from yes to no, the electric switch play of his interior contacts: he consumes himself in relentless self-devouring and his road is a solitary flame.

But as his transformations increase, so they become more violent and painful. Nietzsche's first 'overcoming' is simply to clear out the beliefs held by a little boy and a youth, authoritative opinions, learned by rote or imposed by schooling; these he sheds easily behind him, like an old snake skin. But the more his psychological potency increases, the deeper he must plunge the knife into the inner flesh of his consciousness: the more his convictions become subcutaneous, heavy with anxiety and swollen with blood, the more they are formed from his own plasma, the more brute violence is needed through a profusion of blood and uncompromising severity: this Shylock work, this cutting into the flesh, 'the executioner performing his function on himself'. Ultimately this laying bare of the self reaches the most intimate zone of feeling and here the really dangerous operations are performed; above all the amputation of the Wagner Complex proves an almost fatal surgical intervention in the most vital inner organs, in such close proximity to the heart, a virtual suicide and in its merciless and sudden violence resembles a lust murder, for Nietzsche, at the moment of intimacy, in a ruthless drive for truth, throttles in an amorous embrace the person he loves most and to whom he is closest. But the more violence employed, the better things seem, the more one of these 'overcomings' costs Nietzsche his own blood, the more he lustfully relishes the scrutinizing of the power of his own will; when the indefatigable inquisitor of himself probes each of his own convictions, he experiences a Spanish darkness, a gruesome lust-filled curiosity to contemplate the innumerable auto da fés of ideas now deemed delusional and heretical. Little by little the destruction of himself becomes for Nietzsche an intellectual passion. 'I know the joy of destruction to a degree which is in harmony with my own power to destroy.' From the simple transformation of himself is born the desire to be at variance with himself and to be his own adversary: whole passages in his books bluntly oppose one another. Thus the proselyte (the neophyte) inflamed by his own convictions places a 'yes' after a 'no' and a 'no' after a 'yes'. He extends himself to the infinite, to keep in eternal play the opposing poles of his being and to enjoy, as if the true life of the spirit were there, the electrical tension between them. Perpetual escape and attainment, 'the soul which flees itself and seeks to overtake itself in the widest possible sphere'. This drives him on to the end in an exulted state of madness where such excess proves fatal. For precisely at the moment when the form of his being is stretched to the furthest limits, the tension in his mind snaps: the fiery nucleus, the demonic elemental force explodes and this mighty element annihilates with a single volcanic shockwave the magnificent sequence of structures that his creative mind had raised from his own blood and his life, in the pursuit of the infinite.

VII
Discovery of the South

We need the south at any price,
bright, playful, halcyon and tender tones.

'We aeronauts of the spirit', Nietzsche once declared to vaunt that freedom of thought which found new roads in the boundless untrodden element. And indeed the history of his spiritual wayfaring, his sudden about turns and upturns, that pursuit of the infinite, takes place wholly in a higher space, an inexhaustible spiritual space: like a captive balloon that continually loses ballast, Nietzsche renders himself ever more liberated through his separations and determination to cut adrift. With each cable he severs and each dependency he rejects, he rises higher towards an ever-wider panorama, a more all-encompassing view, a timeless perspective. There are innumerable changes of direction, before the craft drifts into the storm which will destroy it, though we can scarcely count them or identify each one. Only one decisive moment, of crucial significance, shows up clearly and symbolically in Nietzsche's life: the dramatic moment when the last cable is cast off and the free balloon rises from solid earth into free space, passing from gravity into boundless ether. This second in the life of Nietzsche is represented by the moment when he leaves his habitat, his homeland, his professorial chair, his profession, and only returns to Germany in a streaking scornful flight – locating himself from now on in that eternal element of freedom. All that issued from him before that hour barely counts, for the fundamental personality of the later Nietzsche is that which belongs to universal history: the initial changes are merely an exercise in which he seeks to know himself better and without this decisive impulse towards liberty, despite all his spiritual strength, he would have remained locked in a state of subjection; he would have been one of those special-ist professors, an Erwin Rohde, a Dilthey, one of those men we honour in our midst without seeing any revelations for our own spiritual universe. It is only with the emergence of the demonic nature, the release of his intellectual passion, the primordial sense of freedom, that Nietzsche becomes a prophetic figure and transforms his destiny into myth. And while here I am endeav-ouring to present his life not as biography, but as a dramatic act, a work of art and a tragedy of the spirit, for me his genuine work begins at the moment only when the artist emerges in him and he becomes fully conscious of his freedom. Nietzsche in the philologist chrysalis is a subject for philologers: only the winged man, the 'aeronaut of the spirit' belongs in a creative configuration.

The first decisive journey Nietzsche made in his Argonaut search for the self was to the south, and it remains the meta-morphosis of his metamorphoses. Even in Goethe's life the journey to Italy represents the decisive caesura of this kind: he too took refuge in Italy to search out his self, to pass from slavery to liberty and from a virtually vegetative existence to one of creativity. It was he too when crossing the Alps in the first rays of the Italian sun experienced a transformation akin to a volcanic eruption. 'It's as if I had just returned from a journey to Greenland', he writes from Trento. He, too, is 'sick from winter' and in Germany 'suffers under that evil sky'. Seeking the light and a higher clarity, he too feels, as soon as he sets foot on Italian soil, a fundamental upswing in his inner feelings, an expansion and a sense of deliverance. But Goethe experienced too late the miracle of the south, only in his fortieth year; the crust was already too hard around his nature, formed from method and contemplation: a part of his being, of his thought, always remained at home, at court, along with his honours and his obligations. He was already too strongly crystallized in himself to be profoundly modified or transformed by any element. To allow his self to dominate would have been contrary to the organic rule of his life: Goethe always wants to remain master of his destiny and only allows exterior forces to influence him within his own prescribed limits. (While in direct contrast, Nietzsche, Hölderlin, Kleist, those squanderers, always give everything of themselves, with the entirety of their soul, to each impression, content to be once again plunged by them into the broiling eddies of life's river.) In Italy Goethe finds what he is seeking but little else: he seeks there ever deeper attachments, whereas Nietzsche seeks a greater freedom, Goethe seeks the great memories of the past, whereas Nietzsche seeks a magnificent future and the emancipation of all that is historic, Goethe is concerned with what is beneath the earth: ancient art, the Roman eidolon, the mysteries of plant and stone, whereas Nietzsche observes with drunken delight things which are high above him: the sapphire blue sky, the limpid horizon stretching to the infinite, the enchanting streams of light which penetrate every pore. Goethe's experience is primarily cerebral and aesthetic whilst that of Nietzsche is vital. Whilst Goethe's first relationship with Italy is of the artistic kind, Nietzsche discovers a new style of life itself. Goethe is simply enriched whilst Nietzsche is re-rooted and renewed. The man of Weimar, he too seeks renewal ('To be truthful, it might be better for me not to return at all, if I cannot return with a new life'), but like any person half petrified, he only possesses the capacity to experience 'impressions'. For a transformation as radical as Nietzsche's, the fortysomething is already too set in stone, too egotistical and reticent: the powerful and imposing instinct of conservation in his being (which in the final years would take on a glacial and armour-plated rigidity) grants transformation only a limited space alongside stability. The wise dietetic man accepts only what he deems profitable for his nature (whereas the Dionysian type gladly accepts all things in excess and without fear for the danger). Goethe only wants to enrich his possessions, but never will he let himself be lost in them until they have transformed him. That is why his last word on the south is one of carefully weighted and rather measured gratitude, which in spite of everything, displays a whiff of negativity: 'Of all the laudable things I learned in the course of this journey,' he says in his last words relative to Italy, 'you must understand that in no circumstance could I remain alone and exist outside of my homeland.'

If this hard-minted coin is flipped over, Nietzsche's attitude towards the south is shown in stark contrast. His conclusion is the exact opposite of Goethe's, since from now on he could only live alone and outside of his homeland: whilst Goethe on leaving Italy returns to his exact point of departure, having completed an instructive and fascinating journey, bringing back in his luggage, in his heart and mind precious objects for the home, his home. Nietzsche on the other hand is definitively expatriated and only in the south has he located his true self: 'the outlawed prince' is content to be without country, without home or possessions, cut off forever from that 'parochialism of the fatherland', from all 'patriotic subjugation'. From now on, his perspective will be the lofty one of the bird in flight, of 'the good European', of that 'essentially nomadic race of men who exist outside of nations', that race whose advent he senses in the atmosphere, a perspective within which he sets up residence, a realm situated in the beyond, where the future lies. For Nietzsche, where he was born is mere 'history', the place where he 'procreates' now is where the true spiritual master of the house resides. *Ubi pater sum, ibi patria* – 'there where I am father, where I procreate, there is my homeland', and not where he himself was procreated. The unshakeable and inestimable benefit which he draws from his journey to the south, is that from here on the whole world becomes for

Nietzsche both foreign land and homeland and he can uphold this through his gaze of a bird in flight, this glide through the high ether turning his predatory and lucid eye in every direction and beyond the open horizon. (Goethe on the contrary, and in his own words, placed his personality in danger, but always preserved it, by 'enveloping himself in closed horizons'). Once Nietzsche has established himself in the south, he steps definitively beyond his past; he is peremptorily de-Germanized, de-Christianized, he jettisons philology and morality; and nothing characterizes better his excessive nature than this fact: he never once casts a melancholy or regretful look back towards his past. The navigator to the realm of the future is too happy to be embarking on 'the fastest ship for Cosmopolis' to experience any nostalgia for his unilateral, uniform and univocal fatherland. That is why all attempts (currently all the rage) to re-Germanize him should be strongly condemned. For that free man par excellence, there are no more reasons to deny liberty; since he has sensed above him the limpid Italian sky, his soul shivers at the thought of all 'darkening', whether from dull clouds, lecture hall, church or barracks. His lungs, his atmospheric nerves can no longer bear any trace of the north, of that 'Germanic' heaviness: he can no longer live behind fastened windows, behind closed doors, in semi-darkness, in a spiritual twilight and obfuscation. From now on, clarity is king, to see expansively and draw sharp contours to the infinite; and, ever since he has deified this light, with all the fervour of his blood, this primary, dividing, dissecting light of the south, he has renounced forever the 'German devil, the genius, the demon of nebulosity'. His almost gastronomic sensitivity, now he resides in the south, 'abroad', views the overbearing heaviness of German food as an affront to his now refined tastes, a kind of 'indigestion', a non-resolution of a problem, a kind of dragging of the heavy roller of the soul through life: for him the German will never be emancipated enough or 'light' enough. Even the works that he once cherished now leave an intellectual stodginess in the gut. In *The Meistersingers*, he feels something ponderous, convoluted, baroque, a straining towards joviality; in Schopenhauer a clouded viscera, in Kant the hypocritical aftertaste of state morality; in Goethe a leadenness generated by honours and titles, all of them confirming a limited horizon. Everything German is now dusk, half light, obscurity, pervaded by too many shades of the past, too much history, a too heavy burden for the self that he has somehow dragged behind him until now: a mass of possibilities, yet nothing of clarity; incessant questioning, yearning, pining and seeking, a dispiriting and sapping trial, an ongoing vacillation between 'yes' and 'no'. But this anti-German stance is not only a spiritual malaise in the face of new structures of thought erected in that too-new Germany, which had in fact reached its extreme position, not only a political discontent with the 'Empire' and contempt for all those who had sacrificed the German ideal for the canon, not only an aesthetic antipathy towards that Germany of plush upholstery and Berlin victory columns. The new doctrine of the south demands clarity in all problems, not only national ones, demands total commitment to a free-flowing life of clearness and keenness, like that of the sun, 'of the light, just the light, there above even the most wretched things'. The highest ecstasy by way of the highest limpidity – a 'gay science' and not the didactic, pedagogic, tragically bloodless world of the 'scholarly brigade', that patient, dogged objective erudition, that solemn professorial nature of the Germans, who know only the auditorium and the study. His definitive renunciation of the north, of Germany, is not born from his mind, his intellect, but from his nerves, his heart, from feelings and from deep within; it is the cry of freedom from lungs that have re-encountered uncontaminated air, the jubilance of the prisoner who has finally found his 'climate of his soul': liberty. From it comes his innermost rejoicing, the vehement cry of ennoblement: 'I made the leap!'

At the same time as de-Germanizing him, the south also serves to de-Christianize him completely. Whilst like a lizard he enjoys the sun on his back and his soul is lit right through to his innermost nerves, he ponders what exactly had left the world in shadow for so long, made it so anguished, so troubled, so demoralized, so cowardly conscious of sin, what had robbed the most natural, the most serene, the most vital things of their true value, and had prematurely aged what was most precious in the universe, life itself. Christianity is identified as the culprit, for its belief in the hereafter, the key principle that casts its dark cloud over the modern world. This 'malodorous Judaism, con-cocted of Rabbinic doctrines and superstition' has crushed and stifled sensuality, the exhilaration of the world and for fifty gen-erations has been the most lethal narcotic, causing moral para-lysis in what was once a genuine life force. But now (and here he sees his life as a mission), the crusade of the future against the cross has finally begun, the reconquest of the most sacred country of humanity: the life of the world. The 'exuberant sense of vitality', heralds an appreciation for all phenomena of the earth, animal truth and immediacy. Only after his discovery does he notice that the 'red-blooded life' has for years been masked from him by incense and morality. In the south, at this 'great school of spiritual and physical recovery', he learns how to be natural, to be carefree without regrets and to acquire a happy and serene existence, without dread of winter or of a God. His faith is the naive and hearty 'yes' he repeats to himself. But this optimism itself comes from on high, not from a con-cealed God, but from the open armed and generous sun, the light of the south. 'In Saint Petersburg I would be a nihilist, but here I believe like a plant believes, in the sun.' His whole philo-sophy is the direct result of this liberated blood: 'Remain in the south, if only for the sake of faith,' he says to a friend. Now, when clarity is such an effective remedy, it becomes something sacred: and so it was to him and in its name he declared war, the most brutal of his campaigns against all that threatens to lay waste to the brilliancy, serenity, limpidity, the naked truth and the sun-kissed drunkenness of life on earth. 'My relationship with the present age is from now on to be war of knives.'

But with this boldness, a sense of ebullience enters into this inert sickly existence spent behind the shuttered windows of the philologist's life, an upheaval, a stimulus to the congealed blood: the light filters through to the nerves, sets crystalline forms of thoughts in motion and his style, a kind of streaking chameleon-like language, the sun has sparkle like a diamond. Everything is written in 'the language of the thaw' as he himself writes of his first book composed in the south: there is a tone of violent breaking free as when the ice crust melts and spring trickles across a landscape with a playful and ingratiating salaciousness. Light penetrates the last abysses, clarity surrounds the slightest sparkling word, music accompanies every pause and hanging above that halcyon note, a sky filled with radiance. What a transformation from the language of the past, which, though elegantly formed and powerfully arched, was still petrified and now this new high sounding one, so jubilant, supple and buoyant, that loves to employ and strain all its limbs, like Italian with all its expressive gestures, and unlike German which remains incarcerated within a frigid body. It is not in the dignified sonorous voice of the darkly frocked Humanist German, that this new Nietzsche confides those freely hatching thoughts he nets on his walks like so many butterflies; these infant thoughts of freedom demand a new language of freedom, a springing lithesome language with naked gymnastic agility, with subtle articulations, a language that can sprint, leap, rise into the air and descend again, dance all dances, from the melancholy round dance to the rabid tarantella, a language which can bear everything and say everything without a crushing weight on its shoulders and a heavy tread. All the forbearance of the domestic animal, all the sedate dignity has melted away from his style. He whirls in word play to the summits of happiness and in spite of all, still preserves a note of pathos like that of some ancient tolling bell. He brims over with ferment and vigour, from the sparkling champagne fizz of his brief aphorisms he is still capable of frothing over into sudden rhythmic excess. He has around him the golden Falernian light of festiveness, magically transparent, incomparably sunny and joyous. Perhaps never has the language of a German poet been so rapidly, suddenly and completely rejuvenated, and surely no other up to this point had ever been so aglow with the sun, so free, so vinous, so southern, so divinely light of foot, so pagan. Only in the fraternal example of Van Gogh does one witness again the sudden and overwhelming miracle of the sun on a man from the north: only the passage from the mournful grey and brown hues of his Dutch period to the shrill lurid stentorian tones of Provence, only the eruption of that derangement of light in a soul already half blind, can compare to the light obsession the south aroused in Nietzsche's being. Only with these two fanatics of transition is such intoxication, such a frenzied vampire like absorption of light so rapid and unprecedented. Only those possessed by the demon can endure the miracle of that fervid exclusion, right to the very core of their painting, their music, their words.

But Nietzsche's being would not possess the true blood of the demon if he had not allowed himself every possible form of intoxication: which is why he always searches in vain for a superlative for the south and Italy, an 'over light', an 'over clarity'. As Hölderlin gradually edges his Hellas across into 'Asia', that is to say the Oriental, to barbarism, so at the end Nietzsche's passion seethes for the fresh rapture of the tropical, 'the African'. He craves sunburn rather than sunlight, a clarity that cuts cruelly into him, instead of just enclosing things with explicitness, spasms of ecstasy in place of serenity: unflagging is the craving in him for total transformation through the most subtle stimulation of the senses, to turn the dance into a flight and intensify his feeling for existence from red to white hot. And while these desires swell in his veins, language falters before his untamed spirit. It is becoming too narrow, too constrained by substance, too listless. He needs a new element for the Dionysus dance; an even higher freedom than that still subservient to the word – thus he returns to the primeval element, music. The music of the south, his final inspiration, a music where clarity becomes melody and the spirit grows wings. He searches and searches for it, this diaphanous southern music, at all times and in all zones, without ever finding it – until he is obliged to invent his own.

VIII
Refuge of Music

Serenity, oh golden one, come!

Music was there for Nietzsche right from the outset, but it stayed latent, consciously kept at bay by the more powerful will for a spiritual justification. As a child, he impressed his friends with his audacious improvisations and in his juvenile notebooks are found numerous allusions to his own musical compositions. But the more the student is drawn towards philology and then philosophy; the more he stifles this power in his nature, but which still breathes beneath the surface. Music remains for the young man an agreeable respite, a diversion, a pleasure, like the theatre, lectures, riding or fencing, a kind of spiritual gymnastics for the leisure hours. Due to this stringent channelling of interests, this conscious containment, during the early years, not a single note ever filters through to enrich his work: when he writes 'The Birth of tragedy in the spirit of music', music remains to him a mere object, a spiritual theme, but no sense of musical inflection penetrates his language, his poetry or thought. Even the youthful lyrical essays are devoid of all musicality and what is perhaps more surprising still, his attempts at composition, according to Bülow – surely a competent judge – displayed a simple subject matter, an amorphous spirit, typically anti-musical. For a long time music was to him only a private proclivity the young intellectual indulged with irresponsible passion, with the pure blitheness of the dilettante, but always beyond and apart from any 'mission'.

The eruption of music in Nietzsche's inner life only occurs when the crust of philology, the objective erudition which surrounds his life is shed, when the cosmos is shattered and rent by volcanic shockwaves, when the dyke bursts and the tide suddenly surges in. Music always transports with great force those men who are prey to some upheaval, depleted, subjected to violent tensions and torn to their very entrails by some passion; Tolstoy experienced it, as more tragically did Goethe. For even Goethe, who had established a prudent, reserved and rather troubled relationship to music (just as he did to everything that might spell the demonic, for in each transformation he recognized the seducer), succumbed to music in moments of relaxation, (or as he put it: 'in moments of opening out') moments when his whole being is agitated, at times of debilitation and receptiveness. Each time (the last was with Ulrike), he is prey to the feeling he is no longer master of himself, music powerfully engulfs the dam, draws tears from his eyes as tribute, and for music, poetic, joyful, an inadvertent gratitude. Music – and who has not experienced this? – always demands we are in a receptive state, exposed, with a kind of blissful feminine longing to properly garner the fruit of our feelings: that is how it reached Nietzsche at the moment when the south opened up before him, in that carnivorous longing for more life. With curious symbolism it infected him at precisely the moment when his life left the serene, learned phase and passed through sudden catharsis to tragedy; he thought to express *The Birth of Tragedy in the Spirit of Music* and he experienced the very opposite: the *Birth of Music in the Spirit of Tragedy*. The overwhelming potency of new feelings did not suit measured discourse; it aspired to a stronger element, a superior magic: 'You must sing out, oh you my soul.'

Because that demonic wellspring of his being had for so long been blocked by philology, erudition and *taedium vitae**, it now pours forth with so much power and exerts immense liquid

* Weariness of life

pressure, on the innermost fibres of his nervous system, on the final intonation of his style. As if following the infusion of a new vitality, which until then had only embodied things, he suddenly begins to breathe musically: an *andante maestoso* of speech, the ponderous style of his old writings takes on a more sinuous supple 'undulatory' character, the multiple movements of music. All the minor refinements of a virtuoso shine out: the tiny sharp *staccato* of his aphorisms, the *sordino* of the songs, the *pizzicati* of the mockery, the risqué stylizations and harmonies of the prose, the maxims of the poetry. Even the punctuation, the dashes, the pauses and underlining, have all the bearing of musical symbols; never has there been in the German language such a feeling of instrumental prose, or a prose now with a chamber orchestra behind it, now with a full ensemble. An artist of language can find as much pleasure in Nietzsche's polyphony as a musician studying the score of a composer: how many encapsulated and secreted harmonies lie concealed behind the most exaggerated dissonances. How many lucid spiritual forms bask in the rapturous overabundance! For not only are the nervous extremities of the language vibrant with musicality, but the works themselves recall a symphony; their architecture is not coldly intellectual and objective, but issues from a purely musical inspiration. He said himself of *Zarathustra*, that it was written 'In the spirit of the opening movement of the *Ninth Symphony*'; and then the prelude of *Ecce Homo*, unique and truly godlike in terms of language. Are these monumental phrases nothing less than an organ prelude to some colossal cathedral of the future? Poetry like 'Night Song', 'Gondolier Song'; are they not the elemental songs of the human voice amidst its infinite solitude? And in its drunken fervour was it ever so full of dance, so heroic, so Greek as in the paean of his last rejoicing, in the dithyramb of Dionysus? Irradiated on the surface by the limpid light of the south, stirred to his furthest depths by swirls of music, his language becomes liquid and mobile like a wave and in the majestic marine element; Nietzsche's mind performs circles, carrying him into the vortex of his downfall.

Now, as music penetrates him so deeply, Nietzsche, with his alertness to the demon, immediately registers the danger; he senses that this wave could drag him beyond himself. But while Goethe avoided such peril – 'Goethe's prudent attitude towards music', as Nietzsche once noted, he by contrast seizes it by the horns; transformations of values and about turns are his means of defence. And so, (as for his sickness) he makes of it a medicine. Music must be for him now something other than during the years as a philologist. Then he demanded of it an ever-greater tension, a flood of emotion. (Wagner!); its luxuriance and headiness acted as a counterweight to his toneless scholarly existence and proved a stimulant to professorial sterility. But now his thought itself is all excess and ecstasy, he needs music as a kind of psychic bromide, an interior sedative. He has no need to intoxicate himself (for now all that is spiritual is intoxicating), but music is required as 'holy sobriety', as Hölderlin so artfully put it. Music as relaxation, not as excitement. He seeks a music in which to take refuge, when he returns mortally wounded and overwhelmed by fatigue after the chase; he wants to find sanctuary there, a bath, a crystalline wave that cools and purifies: *musica divina,* a music from on high, issuing from the clear sky and not from a soul on heat, suffocating and compressed. A music which will help him forget everything, not a music to draw himself back into crises and catastrophes of feeling, but a music that 'says yes and yes again', a music of the south, clear as the water of its harmonies, natural and pure, a music 'one can whistle'. A music not of chaos (that glows only in itself), but of the seventh day of creation, where all is at rest and where only the spheres praise their God, music as a place of rest. 'Now I have reached a safe harbour, music, music!'

Lightness; that is Nietzsche's last love, his highest measure of all things. What makes him light and gives him health is good: food, spirit, air, sun, landscape, music. What enables him to rise, to forgo the darkness and heaviness of life, the ugliness of truth, that alone is a source of grace. From there comes the belated love of art, as something 'making life possible', as 'the great stimulant of life'. Music, clear, liberating, light, becomes from now on the most cherished refreshment for this fatally anguished mind. During the convulsions of his bloody births, he cannot do without it as a palliative. 'Life without music is simply infirmity and delusion.' Even a man sick with fever, who stretches his cracked and burning lips towards water, cannot know a movement so violent as when he calls for his silvery elixir. 'Did any man ever thirst for music more than I?' It is his last hurrah, his last bid to save him from himself: from it comes the apocalyptic hatred for Wagner, who disturbed the crystalline purity of music with narcotics and stimulants; hence Nietzsche's sufferings realizing 'music's destiny, like an open wound'. The solitary has forsaken all gods; only this one thing does he wish to preserve, his nectar and ambrosia, which refreshes the soul and eternally rejuvenates. 'Art and nothing but art – we have art so that we might not die of truth.' With the desperate claw of the drowning man, he clings to its potency, a power that does not depend on weight, so it might bear him and transport him to its enchanted element.

And music, so harrowingly summoned, inclines towards him and cradles Nietzsche's falling body. All have abandoned the febrile one; friends have long since departed; his thoughts are always of the road, the far distance, on further reckless wanderings; only music is there to accompany him in his final, seventh solitude. What he touches, she touches with him; when he speaks, her clear voice also sounds; forcefully she lifts up he who has weakened prematurely. And when he finally topples into the abyss, she watches over his extinguished soul; Overbeck, who enters the room of the blinded spirit, finds him at the piano, searching out higher melodies with trembling hands and as they carry him home the distracted one sings throughout the entire journey, affecting melodies, his 'Gondolier song'. Into the darkness of the mind music accompanies him, life and death pervaded by her demonic presence.

IX
The Seventh Solitude

A great man is driven on, harried, martyrized
until he shuts himself off in solitude.

'Oh solitude, you my homeland solitude', such is the melancholic song which issues from the glacial world of silence. Zarathustra composes his evening song, which precedes that of the last night, the song of eternal return. For solitude has it not always been the only true residence of he who journeys, his icy hearth, his roof of stone? He found himself in countless cities, he accomplished endless spiritual journeys; often he tried to escape himself by moving to another country; unceasingly he returns to her, wounded, exhausted, disillusioned, to his 'homeland, solitude'.

But whilst she has always travelled with him, the changeable one, she herself has changed and when he looks at her face he is horror-stricken for she has come so much to resemble him after being at such close quarters, harder, more brutal, more violent, just like him; she has learnt how to grieve and grow in the shadow of danger. And if he calls her tenderly, his old dear, familiar solitude, for a long time now she has not been worthy of such names: she has become isolation, the last and seventh solitude, where one is not only alone but abandoned; for around this final Nietzsche there exists a terrifying void, a fearful silence: no hermit, no desert anchorite, no stylite was so forsaken, for all these fanatics of faith still had their God, whose shadow lurks in their hut, or falls from the height of their column. But he, 'the God murderer', had no one at his side, no God or man; the nearer he comes to his self, the further he is distanced from the world, the more his journey lengthens, the more 'the wilderness' spreads around him. Elsewhere the most solitary books slowly and silently begin to exert a powerful magnetic hold over other men: through a nebulous force they draw more into their orbit as a still invisible presence; but Nietzsche's work causes an impression of repulsion; gradually distancing all his friends and isolating him ever more brutally from the present. Each new book costs him a friendship, each work a relationship. Gradually the last crumb of interest towards his conduct dissolves: first he lost the philologists, then Wagner and his spiritual circle, and finally his companions of youth. He could no longer find a publisher in Germany; a hundredweight of texts, the creative production of two decades accumulated chaotically in a cellar; he was obliged to resort to his own meagre funds, those he had so arduously saved or were a gift, to guarantee the appearance of his books. But not only does nobody buy them, even when he gives them away, at the end Nietzsche has no more readers. Of the fourth section of *Zarathustra*, printed at his own expense, he acquires only forty copies and out of the seventy million inhabitants of Germany, he could only find seven people to whom he could send them, so that at peak of his work, he had become a total stranger, inaccessible and foreign to his own epoch. Nobody so much as gives him a crumb of credit, a grain of thanks; on the contrary, just so as not to lose his last friend of youth, Overbeck, he cravenly apologizes for writing books and begs forgiveness. 'Old friend' – we hear his tone of anxiety, we see his lined face, his tense hands, the gestures of someone who has been rejected and fears further blows – 'Do read it from beginning to end, but don't let it torment or disgust you. Summon all your strength in goodwill towards me. If the book seems unbearable to you, at least you might still find a hundred details which are not.' And this is how in the year 1887, the greatest spirit of the century presents to his contemporaries the greatest works of the epoch and he finds nothing more heroic than that to celebrate in a friendship, which nothing can destroy – 'Not even *Zarathustra*', not even *Zarathustra*! – What an endurance test and an embarrassment has Nietzsche's creativity become for those closest to him. How unbridgeable is the distance between his genius and the inferiority of his time. Ever more rarified is the air of his breath, ever more silent, ever more of the void.

This silence turns the last, the seventh solitude of Nietzsche, into a hell: his brain shatters against a wall of metal. 'After a call like my *Zarathustra*, from the very innermost recesses of my being, to not hear a single word of response, nothing, nothing, only immutable solitude multiplied, there is an inconceivable horror in this and even the strongest would perish before it,' he moans one day, adding, 'And I am not the strongest. It sometimes seems to me that I am wounded to death.' But he does not ask for endorsements, applause or glory, quite the contrary, nothing would have suited his warrior temperament better than fury, indignation, mistrust, or even mockery. 'In a state when one is taut as a bow and about to break, any effort is welcome even if it is violent.' He craved any response, whether hot or cold, or even lukewarm, just anything that might actually prove the value of his existence and spiritual life. But even his friends lay aside any long awaited reaction and in their letters skillfully avoid all opinion, as if it might prove too painful. This then is the wound which breaks him, which rankles deep inside him, which festers in his pride, inflames his self awareness, turns his soul gangrenous, 'the wound of no reply'. It alone poisoned his solitude and infected it with fever.

And this fever swells, seething under the surface before suddenly erupting. Observing the writings and letters of Nietzsche's last years, one notes the pulsation of blood as if at a higher altitude: the hearts of Alpine climbers and aviators which are under duress have felt these sharp hammer blows; the last letters of Kleist betray this frenzied hammering, this fraught tone, the ominous roaring and friction noise of a machine about to malfunction. A nervous hot-tempered air undermines Nietzsche's once patient, composed demeanour: 'The long silence has exasperated my pride'. He wants, he demands, now a response at any cost. He harasses the printer of letters and telegrams to advance at breakneck speed, as if any delay would be a serious setback. He cannot wait any longer for his proposed *The Will to Power* to come together as he envisaged it, so he tears it into fragments and hurls them like so many flaming torches into the darkness of his epoch. The 'halcyon tone' has vanished; there are contained in these last works the most unbridled scornful cries of rage and heavy groans of suffering, flayed from his body by the whip of impatience, a savage growling through foaming mouth and bared teeth. He who was once indifferent now declares himself 'exasperated' with provoking his epoch so that they react and let go a howl of rage. To defy them still, he recounts his life in *Ecce Homo,* with a level of cynicism which will enter into universal history. Never has a book exhibited such a craving, such a diseased and feverish convulsion of impatience for response, than the last monumental pamphlets of Nietzsche: like Xerxes insubordinately battling the ocean with a scourge, with insane bravado he wants the indifferent to be stung by the scorpions of his books, to defy the weight of immunity which enshrouds him. There exists in this pressing need for response a demonic anguish, a dread fear of not lasting long enough to see success bloom. And ones senses that with each lash of the whip, he pauses a second and leans outside of himself in horrible suspense, so as to hear the shriek of those struck. But nothing stirs. No response drifts up into the 'azure' solitude. The silence is like an iron clasp around his neck and no cry, not even the most terrible that humanity has ever known can break it. He knows all too well, no god can release him from this prison of the final solitude.

Thus in his last hours an apocalyptic fury seizes his broiling spirit. Like blinded Polyphemus, he bellows and slingshots lumps of rock about him without seeing where they strike, and because he has no one to suffer with him, to feel with him, he can only clutch at his own fluttering heart. He has murdered all gods; so he must make a god of himself. 'Must we ourselves not become gods if we are to appear worthy of such acts?' He has desecrated all altars; so he builds his own altar, *Ecce Homo,* in order to worship himself, he whom nobody worships, in order to celebrate himself, he whom no one celebrates. He piles up the most colossal stones of language; you hear the hammer blows ring out with a force not this century. Enthralled he launches into his dark song of drunkenness and exuberance, the paean to his actions and victories. Darkness is raised over him and it is like that mighty rumble which announces the oncoming storm; then laughter flickers up, a glaring, evil, raving laughter, the gaiety of a desperado that cuts deep into the soul: the hymn of *Ecce Homo*. But the song becomes more volatile, the laughter ever more piercing in the glacial silence and lost in his own entrancement he lifts his hands, dithyrambic his foot twitches: and suddenly the dance begins, the dance around the abyss, the abyss of his own downfall.

X
Dance over the Abyss

If you stare for a long time into the abyss
the abyss will stare back at you

The five months of autumn 1888, the final creative phase, are unique in the annals of literary productivity. Never before in such a brief period has a genius thought in such an intensive, complete, radical and hyperbolic manner, nor was an earthly mind so invaded with ideas, flooded with images and music than this one designed by fate. With this superabundance, this ecstasy of drunken effusion, this fanatical furor of creation, the history of the spirit offers no comparable example. Only perhaps when in the same year, in the same climate, a painter hounded by madness experiences an equally accelerated productivity, in an Arles garden of an insane asylum, Van Gogh paints with the same rapidity, with the same obsessive desire for light, with the same maniacal superfluity for creation. Barely has he put the final touches to one of his blistering white canvases, than he is applying his flawless strokes to another, no hesitation, no plan, no reflection. His creation is as if dictated, a demonic divination and rapidity of perception, an unbroken continuity of visions. Friends who left Van Gogh at his easel an hour before, are astonished to find on their return that he has already completed a second picture, then without pausing for breath and with caked brush and inflamed eyes, he is starting on a third: the demon that has him by the throat grants him no breath, no intermission, indifferent is the wild rider of the panting fervid body wrecked beneath him. In exactly the same way Nietzsche creates work after work, without respite, without taking a breath, with the same clairvoyance and velocity. Ten days, fifteen days, three weeks, these are the durations of his last works: conception, gestation, delivery, presentation and final drafting, streaking past like a comet. No incubation period, no research time, no tentative investigations, amendments or corrections, all is immediately perfect, definitive, unchangeable, scalding hot and chilled to the bone at the same time. Never has a brain endured such a permanently high electric tension as in those last convulsions of his words; never have associations of words been formed at such magic speeds; vision is at one with language, the idea is supreme clarity and in spite of this massive surplus, one feels no sense of exertion or effort – creation has for a long time now ceased to be an activity, a task, it is simply laissez-faire, an incidence of the higher powers. He whose spirit resonates in him merely needs to lift his eyes, eyes that penetrate the outer distances and 'think far', and (like Hölderlin, in his last momentum towards mythical contemplation) he notices vast stretches of time in past and future: only he who has the demon of clear-sightedness sees them close-up with demonic sharpness. He has only to stretch out his hand, his hot swift hand, to seize them; and barely has he seized them than they have blossomed into images, resonating with music, animated and vital. And this onrush of ideas and images is not interrupted even for a second on these truly Napoleonic days. The spirit is invaded, undergoes an elemental violence. '*Zarathustra* has attacked me'; always wild surprise and a state of being where he finds himself defenceless against something far more powerful than himself – as if somewhere in his soul a secret dam of reason and organic resistance had been breached by a torrent that now sends its rapids over this impotent being, deprived of all strength of will. 'Perhaps never before has anything been created with such an excess of power,' declares Nietzsche ecstatically, of his last works; but never does he dare admit it is his own strength acting on him and destroying him. On the contrary, he sees himself as intoxicated – piously imagining that

80

he is merely the 'mouthpiece for an otherworldly imperative', and that he is divinely possessed by a superior demonic element.

But who could describe the event, this miracle of inspiration, the terrors and tremors of this uninterrupted storm of production over five months, but he himself, in an exuberance of gratitude, in that force illuminated by the power of all he has experienced. Now all we can do is copy out his lines crossed by their forks of lightning.

Has anyone at the close of the nineteenth century any clear idea of what the poets of more powerful epochs called inspiration? If not, then allow me to describe it. Whatever grain of superstition may still dwell in the mind, we should dismiss the idea that we are not the incarnation, the mouthpiece, the medium for higher forces. The notion of revelation, in the sense that suddenly, with indescribable certainty and indefinable subtlety, something becomes visible, audible, something that overwhelms and moves you at the very limits of your self, is a stark fact. We listen, we do not seek; we assume, we do not ask who gives; like lightening a thought lights you, with necessity in its wavering form – I had no choice. A rapture whose terrific tension is reduced by a flood of tears, where unconsciously the tread, sometimes speeds up and sometimes slows down, a state beyond oneself where one is so conscious of countless tense quiverings to the tips of the toes: a depth of happiness where the union of pain and darkness is not seen in contradiction but as conditional, deified, the primary colour at the heart of such an overflowing of light: an instinct for rhythmical relationships, the vast expanses of exaggerated forms – the length, the need for a comprehensive rhythm, virtually the gauge of inspirational power, which partially compensates for the pressure and tension inflicted... Everything takes place at the highest sphere of the involuntary, in a whirlpool of free feeling, indetermination, power, the divine… Most remarkable is the involuntary character of the image, of parables: we no longer have any idea what an image or parable is, all presents itself as the most immediate, the most right, the plainest expression, it really appears, recalling *Zarathustra*, that things come to offer themselves as a parable. 'Here at your oration, all things come, caressing and flattering you: for they want to ride upon your wing. With each parable you fly towards a truth. Language and its shrine open to you; all being wants to be language, all being wants you to learn how to speak it…' Such is my experience of inspiration; I have no doubt that you would have to go back a thousand years to find someone else who could say to me: Yes and it is mine too.

In such a tone of vertiginous rapture, in this hymn addressed to himself, I accept that doctors today might diagnose a state of euphoria, the last delirious outpourings of one who is about to expire, the stigmata of megalomania, that exaltation of the self which is common to all spirits in malaise. But I would ask, when has the state of creative intoxication left for eternity structures of such adamantine clarity? For it is there the uncanny and unprecedented miracle of Nietzsche's last works: the high levels of lucidity alongside the highest levels of somnambulistic delirium, like serpents, with their bestial and bacchanal power coiled side by side. Usually the exalted, all those whose souls Dionysus has intoxicated, speak through heavy lips and their words seem dark and obscure. As in a dream their expressions are momentous and convoluted; all those who have stared into the abyss have this mysterious Orphic Pythian tone of the language of elsewhere, of which our sense has only a dread presentiment and our spirit limited understanding. Nietzsche however, is clear as a diamond in his exaltation and his language remains uncorrupted, hard and incisive. Perhaps no one has ever been so awake and alert, so free from opaqueness and so lucid, inclining over the abysm of madness: Nietzsche's expression is not (as with Hölderlin, the mystics and pythians) coloured and darkened by mystery; on the contrary, he is never so sharply defined as in those last hours, you might say he is illuminated by mystery. It is true that the light that shines on him is an ominous one; it has that fantastical sickly radiance of a summer midnight, that reddish glow suspended over an iceberg, a northern light of the soul that in its unique grandeur brings a shiver. It does not warm – it strikes horror. It does not dazzle – it annihilates. Nietzsche is not dragged to the abyss by undulating rhythms of feeling like Hölderlin, nor by a wave of melancholy: he is consumed by his own light, more by a bolt of light, a sun burning and radiating to excess, by a blazing exhilaration no longer possible to endure. Nietzsche's disintegration is a kind of death by light, an incineration of the spirit by its own flame.

For a long time these profligate lucidities had set his heart beating faster and kept the fire stoked; but with his mystical prescience he is often terrified of this abundance of light from on high and the wild carousing of his soul. 'The intensities of my feelings make me shudder and laugh.' But nothing can curb this current of rhapsody, this excess of thoughts dropping down from on high like falcons that rustle around him, jangling and ringing, day and night, night and day, hour on hour, until his blood seems fit to burst through his temples. Through the night the chloral calms him, erecting a flimsy canopy of sleep against the pelting downpour of visions. But his nerves are red-hot threads of metal: his whole body becomes electricity and light, a blistering, sparkling, fulgurant, shimmering light.

Is it any wonder that in this vortex of high velocity inspirations, in this unceasing stream of vertiginous thoughts, Nietzsche loses his footing on earth and, fatally mauled by all the demons of the mind, no longer knows who he is and adrift in a limitless space no longer knows any limit? For a long time now (ever since he felt he obeyed the directives of a higher power rather than his own self) his hand has wavered from signing letters in his own name: Friedrich Nietzsche. For the grandson of a protestant pastor of Naumburg has the sensation that it is not he who is living through these extraordinary events but another being who has no name as yet, a superior power, a new martyr for humanity. Which is why he only signs his last letters with symbolic names such as: 'The Monster', 'The Crucified', 'The Anti-Christ', 'Dionysus', sensing that he is no longer a man, but a higher being on a mission. 'I am not a man, I am dynamite.' 'I am an event in world history, that cleaves in two the story of humanity.' He cries out with monumental hubris into the horrifying silence. Just like Napoleon in Moscow as it burns, facing the Russian winter while all about him lie the miserable remnants of the most powerful armies, still issues the most grandiose and menacing proclamations (grandiose to the point of ridicule), Nietzsche in the flaming Kremlin of his brain composes impotently, with the debris of his thoughts, the most outrageous pamphlets: he orders that the German emperor go to Rome in order to be shot; he invites the European powers to undertake military action against Germany, to encircle the Fatherland in a ring of steel. Never has such an apocalyptic fury been launched more ardently into the void, never has such magnificent megalomania propelled the spirit above all earthly matters. His words resound like hammer blows against the world's edifice: he demands that the calendar be amended and begin not with the birth of Christ, but from the appearance of his anti-Christ; he places his image above all those of previous epochs, even a sick Nietzsche's derangement is greater than in those whose spirits are blinded; here too as elsewhere, the most glorious morbid excess reigns in him.

Never has a creator been assaulted by such a storm surge of inspiration as Nietzsche was during that single autumn. 'No one has written, felt, suffered to this extent before. Only a god, a Dionysus suffers to this extent.' These words declared at the onset of his illness are horrifyingly true. For that small second floor room in Sils-Maria, those cave lodgings sheltered a sick man whose nerves were shot but still gave rise to the most courageous thoughts, the most magnificent words that the closing century had known. The creative genie took refuge under this low roof burned by the sun and spread its opulence over this poor solitary man, nameless, withdrawing and lost, to an extent no human being has ever experienced. And in this constricted space, overcome by the expanses beyond, the daunted one, his earthly soul reeling and groping beneath the hammer blows of lightning bolts, feels the whip of inspiration and proclamation. Just like the spiritually blinded Hölderlin, he senses that a god is above him, a fiery god, whose gaze is impossible to bear and whose breath consumes him... Always the trembling one rises to search his face and watch the thoughts spill chaotically from him... For he who feels, who literally 'creates' and suffers unutterable torments... is he not – is he not himself, God...? Is he not a new God of the universe, since he killed off the old one...? Who is he, the crucified, the dead god or the new living one...? The God of his youth, Dionysus, or is he at the same time the crucified Dionysus...? Such thoughts hound him, burning urgently in a profusion of light... but is there still light? Or is it now music? The little room on the fourth floor of the via Alberto begins to resound, all the spheres gleam and quiver, all the skies are transformed... Oh what music: hot tears run down into his whiskers... Oh what divine tenderness... what smaragdina* joy... and now, this superb clarity... and down there in the street the people are smiling... look how they rise to salute to him... that's why the grocer felt around in his basket for the best apples

* Emerald in colour

to give him... everything bows to him the murderer of God, all is in celebration, in jubilation... but why? Well, he knows well enough! Because the anti-Christ is here and everyone is chanting Hosanna! Hosanna! Everything resounds, the world resounds with buoyancy and music... and then suddenly all goes quiet... something has fallen... it is him... in front of the house... someone helps him up... now here he is back in his room... had he been sleeping long? It seems so dark... the piano is there; music... Music! Then suddenly people in the room... isn't that Overbeck?... but surely he was in Basel... and he himself, he is... where?... he no longer knows... why are they all gazing at him so strangely, with such concern?... then a carriage, a carriage... how the rails rustle strangely... you would think they were singing... yes they are singing... the 'Gondolier Song' and he sings along with them... and he sings on into eternal darkness.

Then for a long time now, somewhere else, a darkened room, without sunlight. No more light either inside or out. Somewhere around him men are still in conversation. A woman – is that not his sister? But surely she is far away, far away in the land of the Lamas – she reads to him from books... books? Had he not once written books? Someone responds to him with tenderness. He no longer understands what they are saying. One whose spirit has suffered such a tempest is now forever deaf to all human words. One whose eye was stared into so deeply by the demon is from now on blind.

XI
Educator of Freedom

Greatness: to give direction

'They will understand me after the next European war.' This prophetic phrase is to be found amongst Nietzsche's last writings. We can only grasp the true sense of his words having now experienced the state of tension, uncertainty and danger of our world at the turn of the last century: it seems that in this genius of the atmospheric, whose nerves read in the closeness of the air the oncoming storm, who transformed prescience into language, the unburdening of the entire moral weight of Europe is felt; thus we are present at the mightiest storm of the spirit preceding the most destructive storm in history. Nietzsche's 'far-searching gaze' sees the crisis advancing, and whilst others complaisantly warm themselves at the hearth of verbiage, he confirms the cause: 'The nationalist heart pruritus* and blood poisoning of the peoples of Europe, cordoning them off from each other as if in quarantine.' 'The horned cattle nationalism', devoid of higher thought, with only a selfishness drawn slavishly from history, when all natural forces are frantically propelling them towards a higher future. And the declaration of catastrophe issues with fury from his lips, when he views the convulsive attempts to 'make permanent in Europe a network of small states', merely to prop up a morality that rests only on business interests and commerce. 'This absurd situation cannot go on much longer,' inscribes his fiery finger on the wall. 'The ice beneath us is already too thin: we all sense the warm and dangerous breeze heralding the thaw.' No one felt as keenly as

* Itch, irritation

Nietzsche the augural cracking of the European edifice; no one in an optimistic epoch so contented with itself, cried out to Europe with so much despair, to flee, to flee in lucidity and veracity, to take refuge in the realm of a higher intellectual freedom above Europe's drawn-out scream. No one felt so keenly that an epoch was approaching extinction and that in the midst of this deadly crisis something new was straining to evolve: but only now do we know what he knew.

This deadly crisis he fatally sensed and fatally endured in advance: that is his heroism and greatness. And the massive tension which stretched his spirit to the limit, and finally broke it into pieces, united him with a superior element; it was nothing less than the febrile state of our world before the abscess bursts. The storm birds, messengers of the spirit, announce by their flight the great revolutions and catastrophes and there is some truth in that belief of a people who, before wars and crises, see comets blazing their bloody trail across the heavens. Nietzsche was such a beacon in the high ether, the summer lightning ahead of the thunderstorm, the great boom unleashed from the mountain summits before the storm sinks into the valleys; no one else sensed in advance with such climatic assuredness and to the last detail, the violence of the cataclysm (disintegration) stalking our culture. There is the eternal tragedy of the spirit, that his sphere of lucidity and higher thought could not communicate with the heavy sluggish air of his time, that the present always remains disregardful when above it a sign glides across the heavens and the soughing of the wings of prophesy is heard. But even the most lucid genius of the century was not clear enough for his time to be understood: like that out-of-breath Marathon runner, who, having witnessed the downfall of the Persian Empire, runs the many miles to Athens with bursting lungs, only to manage an ecstatic shriek (after which he is felled by a haemorrhage from a fatally overtaxed chest), so Nietzsche proclaims the apocalypse facing our culture but cannot avert it. He can only launch a mighty unforgettable exhilarated cry to his epoch: then his mind breaks apart.

For me it is Jacob Burckhardt, the most astute reader of Nietzsche, who best defines his message, when he wrote that his books 'Increased independence in the world'. This shrewd and erudite man wrote: 'Independence *in* the world, not independence *of* the world', since independence exists solely with the individual and does not grow out of numbers: nor does it increase with books and culture: 'There is no heroic age, only heroic men.' Only the individual can bring independence to the world and always for himself alone. For each free spirit is an Alexander. He impetuously conquers all provinces and kingdoms, but he has no inheritor; always a free empire is prey to Diadochi and their lackeys, to commentators and interpreters, slaves to the written word. Nietzsche's monumental independence does not bear the gift of a doctrine (as the pedagogues imagine), but an atmosphere, a clear atmosphere of higher lucidity permeated by passion, of a demonic nature, which discharges itself only in storms and destruction. On contact with his works one tastes the ozone, a primal air, loosed of all weight, of all obscurity and heaviness; one sees clearly in this heroic landscape to the summits of the sky and one breathes an uncommon air, transparent and vital, an air for robust hearts and free spirits. Freedom is always the ultimate sensation for Nietzsche – the *raison d'être* of his life and that of his downfall. Just as nature has need of hurricanes and cyclones to give free reign to its excess of force in a violent revolt against its own stability, so the spirit has need from time to time of a man possessed by the demon, whose higher power is raised against the community of thought and the monotony of morality. Men who destroy and destroy themselves at the same time; but such heroic firebrands are no lesser creators and artists of the universe, than the muted architects. If some expose the plenitude of life, others will demonstrate its inconceivable scale. Only tragic natures can transport us to the furthest depths of feeling and only the immeasurable allows humanity to recognize their own dimensions.

Landscape of Sils-Maria

Acknowledgements

I would like to express my gratitude to the Nietzsche Haus in Sils-Maria Switzerland for their generous assistance with this project. I am grateful to them for supplying the period photos of Nietzsche and allowing me to stay at various periods under the roof of that legendary residence, not least the memorable night spent in Nietzsche's room beside a giant plaster cast of his moustache. Thank you to Mr Joachim Jung, Prof. Dr Peter André Bloch and most of all Dr Peter Villwock. I would also like to thank Julia Rosenthal for her support and enthusiasm.

The Nietzsche Haus – Sils Maria

Nietzsche's room in the Nietzsche Haus

IN DIESEM HAUSE WOHNTE
FRIEDRICH NIETZSCHE
WÄHREND SCHAFFENSREICHER
SOMMERMONATE 1881-1888

54

Plaque on the Nietzsche Haus

A Note on the Photographs

The period photographs of Nietzsche are taken from the collection at the museum of the Nietzsche Haus in Sils-Maria, Switzerland, though the originals are held in different archives in Germany. For example the now famous final images of Nietzsche, 'Der kranke Nietzsche', taken by Hans Olde during the summer of 1899, are held by the Goethe und Schiller Archive in Weimar. Olde, a noted artist visited Nietzsche in the Villa Silberblick in Weimar between June and August 1899 with the intention of drawing his portrait, but he also took a handful of photographs of the invalided philosopher. These haunting images show a lean-faced Nietzsche looking worn out and haggard, chair- or couch-bound and swathed in blankets. Nietzsche possesses a vacant look and has an uncanny stillness about him, his pupils are slightly raised and one thin hand rests limply on the blanket. All the evidence suggests that here is a man who has endured prolonged sufferings and has succumbed to a fatal exhaustion. Even without knowing anything about the figure in these images, the tragedy of individual human disintegration is manifest.

The landscape photo of the Engadine plateau, the lake of Sils (Silsersee) and its reflected mountains was included to give a pictorial example of the grandeur and purity of the unique landscape surrounding Sils-Maria, where Nietzsche wrote prodigiously over several summers during the 1880s and which proved the only landscape where he found both high levels of inspiration and solace. The inscription on the rock known as 'Zarathustra's roundelay' is found at the tip of the narrow Chastè peninsula which leads out into the lake, and where Nietzsche loved to walk, his dream being to have a house constructed here midway between the two surrounding mountain ranges and with water on either side. The rock with the roundelay should not be confused with the so-called 'Zarathustra stone' which lies on the southern edge of the Silvaplana lake near Surlej, so named for it was here, as he beheld this rock on one of his perambulations around the lake, that Nietzsche was said to have conceived the notion of 'Eternal Recurrence'. The remaining photos show the Nietzsche Haus as it is today, Nietzsche's room, now an exhibit within a museum which contains amongst other relics, a cast of his death mask, and a small library holding notably the Nietzsche collection of Dr Oscar Levy (1867–1946), who oversaw the first complete edition of his works in English.

Zarathustra's roundelay (Translation R.J. Hollingdale)

O man! Attend!
What does deep midnight's voice contend?
'I slept my sleep,
'And now awake at dreaming's end:
'The world is deep,
'And deeper than day can comprehend.
'Deep is its woe,
'Joy—deeper than heart's agony:
'Woe says: Fade! Go!
'But all joy wants eternity,
'Wants deep, deep, deep eternity!'

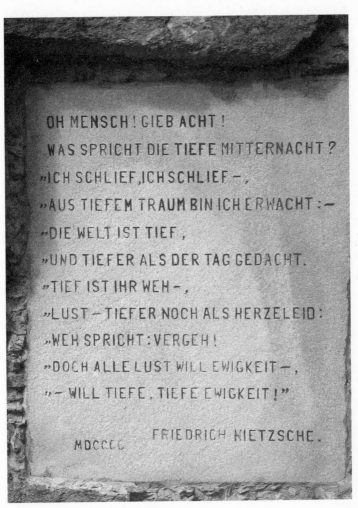

The Nietzsche stone with Zarathustra's roundelay

Biographical Note

Will Stone, born 1966, is a poet, literary translator and essayist, who divides his time between the UK and Belgium. His previous books for Hesperus Press include *Journeys* by Stefan Zweig (2010) and *Rilke in Paris* by Maurice Betz (2012). Will's first collection of poems *Glaciation*, from Salt Publishing (2007), won the international Glen Dimplex Award for poetry in 2008. His second collection of poems *Drawing in Ash*, was also published by Salt in May 2011 and the third entitled *The Sleepwalkers*, will be published in early 2014 with Rufus Books. His published translations of poetry include *To The Silenced – Selected Poems of Georg Trakl* (Arc Publications, 2005) and the sonnet sequence *Les Chimères* by Gérard de Nerval (Menard Press, 1999). Arc will publish two collections of Selected Poems by long neglected francophone Belgian poets Emile Verhaeren and Georges Rodenbach in their first modern English translations, in spring 2013.

Will has contributed reviews, essays, poems and translations to a number of literary journals and magazines in the UK and abroad, including the *Times Literary Supplement*, *The London Magazine*, *The Edinburgh Review*, *Poetry Review*, *Irish Pages*, *The Black Herald* and *The White Review*. His future projects include a further title for Hesperus, Joseph Roth – *On the end of the world,* journalistic pieces written during the writer's exile in Paris during the thirties, a translation of Maeterlinck's influential first collection of poems *Serres Chaudes* or 'Hothouses' (1889), an expanded edition of Georg Trakl's poetry and *The Undisclosed Anatomy of Belgium,* a collection of his own essays which constitute a psycho-geographical personal exploration of lesser known aspects of the country's landscape, history, literature and art.

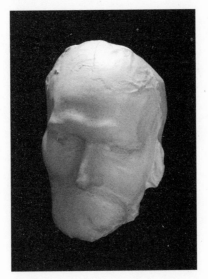

Nietzsche's death mask

HESPERUS PRESS

Hesperus Press is committed to bringing near what is far –
far both in space and time. Works written by the greatest
authors, and unjustly neglected or simply little known in
the English-speaking world, are made accessible through
new translations and a completely fresh editorial approach.
Through these classic works, the reader is introduced to the
greatest writers from all times and all cultures.

For more information on Hesperus Press, please visit our
website: **www.hesperuspress.com**

SELECTED TITLES FROM HESPERUS PRESS

Author	Title	Foreword writer
Pietro Aretino	*The School of Whoredom*	Paul Bailey
Pietro Aretino	*The Secret Life of Nuns*	
Jane Austen	*Lesley Castle*	Zoë Heller
Jane Austen	*Love and Friendship*	Fay Weldon
Honoré de Balzac	*Colonel Chabert*	A.N. Wilson
Charles Baudelaire	*On Wine and Hashish*	Margaret Drabble
Giovanni Boccaccio	*Life of Dante*	A.N. Wilson
Charlotte Brontë	*The Spell*	
Emily Brontë	*Poems of Solitude*	Helen Dunmore
Mikhail Bulgakov	*Fatal Eggs*	Doris Lessing
Mikhail Bulgakov	*The Heart of a Dog*	A.S. Byatt
Giacomo Casanova	*The Duel*	Tim Parks
Miguel de Cervantes	*The Dialogue of the Dogs*	Ben Okri
Geoffrey Chaucer	*The Parliament of Birds*	
Anton Chekhov	*The Story of a Nobody*	Louis de Bernières
Anton Chekhov	*Three Years*	William Fiennes
Wilkie Collins	*The Frozen Deep*	
Joseph Conrad	*Heart of Darkness*	A.N. Wilson
Joseph Conrad	*The Return*	Colm Tóibín
Gabriele D'Annunzio	*The Book of the Virgins*	Tim Parks
Dante Alighieri	*The Divine Comedy: Inferno*	
Dante Alighieri	*New Life*	Louis de Bernières
Daniel Defoe	*The King of Pirates*	Peter Ackroyd
Marquis de Sade	*Incest*	Janet Street-Porter
Charles Dickens	*The Haunted House*	Peter Ackroyd
Charles Dickens	*A House to Let*	
Fyodor Dostoevsky	*The Double*	Jeremy Dyson
Fyodor Dostoevsky	*Poor People*	Charlotte Hobson
Alexandre Dumas	*One Thousand and One Ghosts*	